Name:

Age:

Date:

WRITE   Color   Doodle

READ

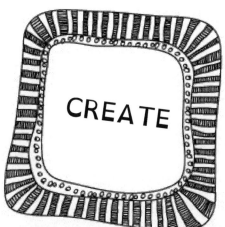

CREATE

Spell

Explore

JOY

READ

LEARN

DISCOVER

ORGANIZE

DRAW

How to Use this Book

LIST EIGHT THINGS - That you want to learn about:

1.

2.

3.

4.

5.

6.

7.

8.

Action Steps:

1. Go to the library or bookstore.

2. Bring home a stack of at least eight interesting books and movies about these topics. Choose some books that have diagrams, instructions and illustrations.

Supplies Needed:

You will need pencils, colored pencils, pens and markers. If learning from YouTube you need internet and a viewing device.

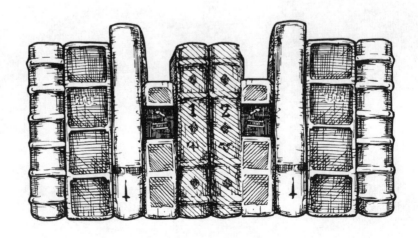

Choose EIGHT Books To Use As School Books!

1. Write down the titles on each cover below.
2. Keep your stack of books in a safe place.
3. Be ready to read a few pages from your books daily.
4. Complete 5 or 6 pages each day in this workbook.

This page is for other books that you may use.

1. Write down the titles on each cover below.
2. Keep your stack of books in a safe place.
3. Be ready to read a few pages from your books daily.
4. Complete 5 or 6 pages each day in this workbook.

Circle Today's Date

January
February
March
April
May
June
July
August
September
October
November
December

1 2 3 4 5 6
7 8 9 10 11
12 13 14 15
16 17 18 19
20 21 22 23
24 25 26 27
28 29 30 31

MONDAY
TUESDAY
WEDNESDAY
THURSDAY
FRIDAY
SATURDAY
SUNDAY

2015
2016
2017
2018
2019
2020
2021
2022
2023
2024
2025
2026
2027
2028
2029

Write Today's Date: _ _ _ _ _ _ _ _ _ _ _ _ _ _ _ _

Write down an inspirational quote:

My Goals

To-Do List

_____
_____
_____
_____
_____
_____

Nature Study

Go outside and make a realistic
drawing of something you find in
in nature.

Reading Time - 1 Hour

Choose Four Books - Read from each book for 15 minutes.

Copy a sentence or picture from each book here:

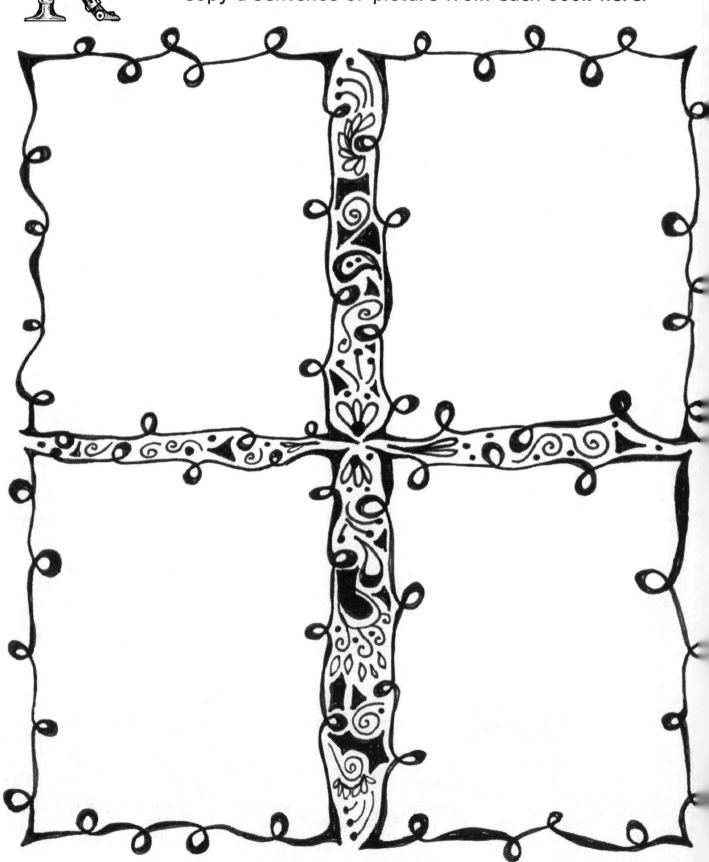

Observation Time

Look at the object in the picture.

Do you know what it is?

Yes / No / Unsure

Write down four facts or observations
about the object.

1. _____
2. _____
3. _____
4. _____

Emotions & Moods

How are your feeling today?
Color the facial expressions
to match today's moods.

Can you of three things that might help your mood improve?

1.
2.
3.

Circle Today's Date

January
February
March
April
May
June
July
August
September
October
November
December

1 2 3 4 5 6
7 8 9 10 11
12 13 14 15
16 17 18 19
20 21 22 23
24 25 26 27
28 29 30 31

MONDAY
TUESDAY
WEDNESDAY
THURSDAY
FRIDAY
SATURDAY
SUNDAY

2015
2016
2017
2018
2019
2020
2021
2022
2023
2024
2025
2026
2027
2028
2029

Write Today's Date: _ _ _ _ _ _ _ _ _ _ _ _ _ _ _

Spelling Time

Find 20 Words with **4** letters each.
Look in your books for words.
Write the words here:

_____   _____

_____   _____

_____   _____

_____   _____

_____   _____

_____   _____

_____   _____

_____   _____

_____   _____

Film Study

Watch a Documentary, Educational Program, Movie, or YouTube Tutorial.

TITLE:

TIME:

TOPIC: _____

I learned:_____

_____

_____

_____

NOTES:

Draw a Scene From the Film:

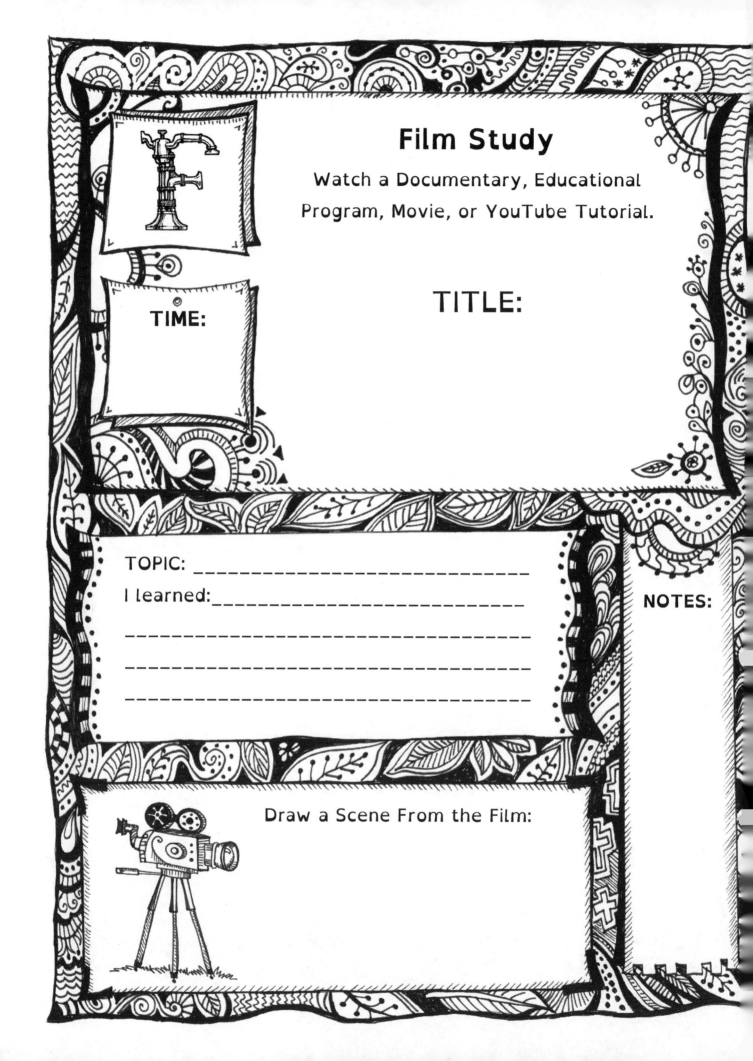

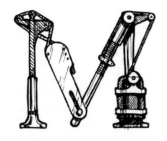

Math Practice

You can design something. You can make
graphs, maps, or geometric designs.
You can practice math problems.

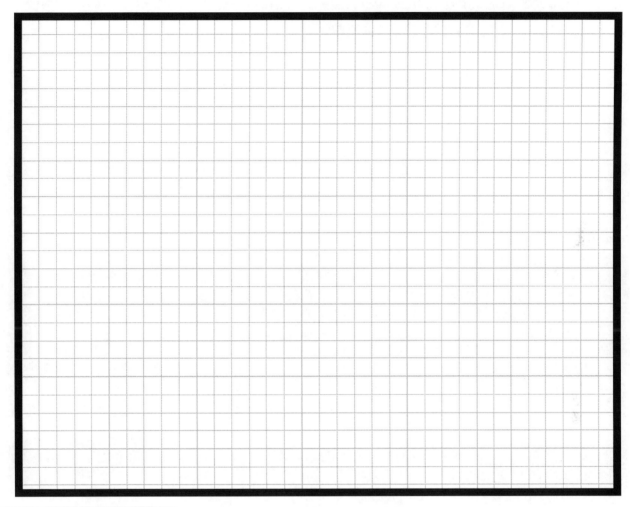

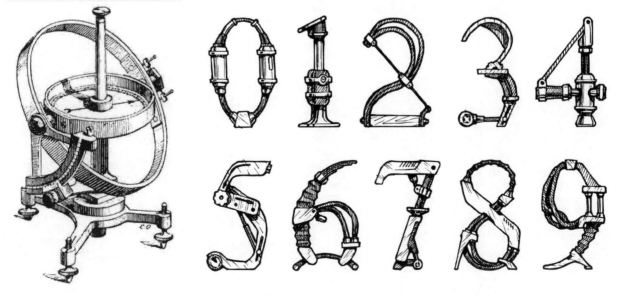

World News Today!

Talk to your parents about current events.

Look at a newspaper, news broadcast or website.

Color the countries your learn about.

Tell the news stories with words or pictures.

Copywork

Find an interesting paragraph in one of your books and copy it. Be diligent to make your writing look exactly like it does the book.

TITLE:_____

Page Number:_____

_____

_____

_____

_____

_____

_____

_____

_____

_____

Creative
Coloring Time

Circle Today's Date

January
February
March
April
May
June
July
August
September
October
November
December

1 2 3 4 5 6
7 8 9 10 11
12 13 14 15
16 17 18 19
20 21 22 23
24 25 26 27
28 29 30 31

MONDAY
TUESDAY
WEDNESDAY
THURSDAY
FRIDAY
SATURDAY
SUNDAY

2015
2016
2017
2018
2019
2020
2021
2022
2023
2024
2025
2026
2027
2028
2029

Write Today's Date: _____

Write down an inspirational quote:

My Goals

To-Do List

_____
_____
_____
_____
_____
_____

Nature Study

Go outside and make a realistic
drawing of something you find in
in nature.

Observation Time

Look at the object in the picture.

Do you know what it is?

Yes / No / Unsure

Write down four facts or observations
about the object.

1. _____
2. _____
3. _____
4. _____

Emotions & Moods

How are your feeling today?
Color the facial expressions
to match today's moods.

Can you of three things that might help your mood improve?

1.
2.
3.

Reading Time - 1 Hour

Choose Four Books - Read from each book for 15 minutes.

Copy a sentence or picture from each book here:

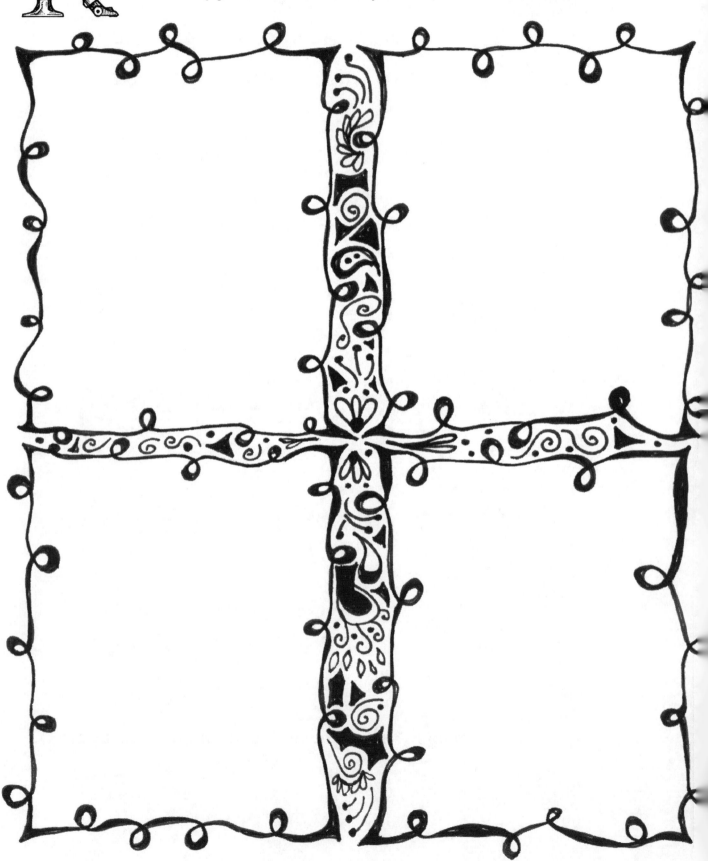

Circle Today's Date

January
February
March
April
May
June
July
August
September
October
November
December

1 2 3 4 5 6
7 8 9 10 11
12 13 14 15
16 17 18 19
20 21 22 23
24 25 26 27
28 29 30 31

MONDAY
TUESDAY
WEDNESDAY
THURSDAY
FRIDAY
SATURDAY
SUNDAY

2015
2016
2017
2018
2019
2020
2021
2022
2023
2024
2025
2026
2027
2028
2029

Write Today's Date: _____

Spelling Time

Find 20 Words with 5 letters each.
Look in your books for words.
Write the words here:

_____   _____

_____   _____

_____   _____

_____   _____

_____   _____

_____   _____

_____   _____

_____   _____

_____   _____

_____   _____

Film Study

Watch a Documentary, Educational Program, Movie, or YouTube Tutorial.

TIME:

TITLE:

TOPIC: _____

I learned: _____

_____

_____

_____

NOTES:

Draw a Scene From the Film:

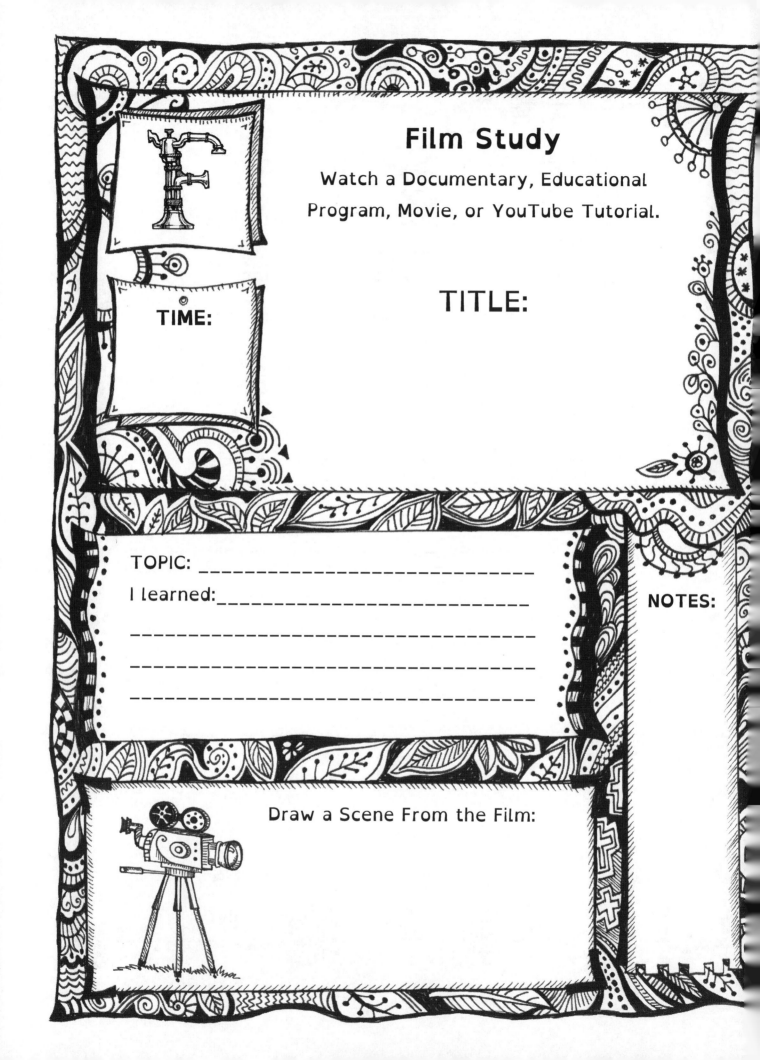

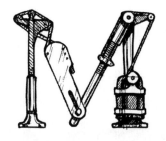

Math Practice

You can design something. You can make graphs, maps, or geometric designs. You can practice math problems.

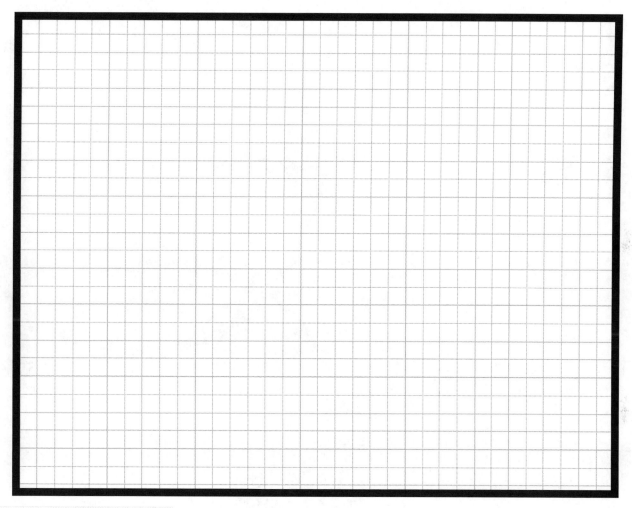

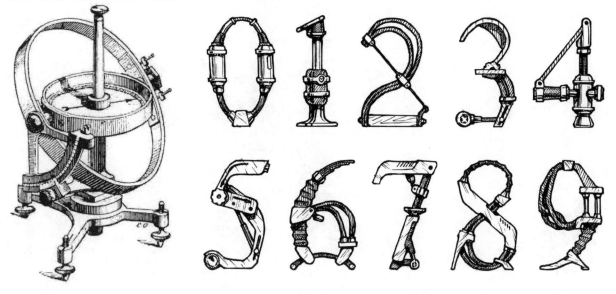

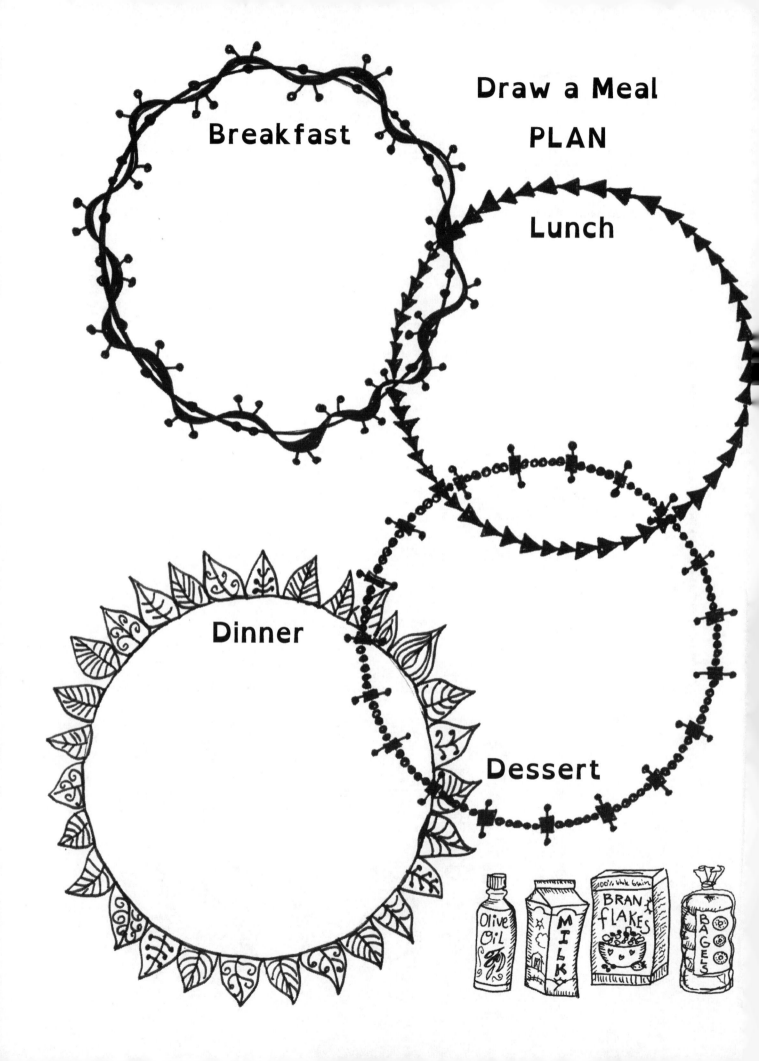

Copywork

Find an interesting paragraph in one of your books and copy it. Be diligent to make your writing look exactly like it does the book.

TITLE:_____

Page Number:_____

_____

_____

_____

_____

_____

_____

_____

_____

_____

_____

 Creative
Coloring Time

Circle Today's Date

January
February
March
April
May
June
July
August
September
October
November
December

1 2 3 4 5 6
7 8 9 10 11
12 13 14 15
16 17 18 19
20 21 22 23
24 25 26 27
28 29 30 31

MONDAY
TUESDAY
WEDNESDAY
THURSDAY
FRIDAY
SATURDAY
SUNDAY

2015
2016
2017
2018
2019
2020
2021
2022
2023
2024
2025
2026
2027
2028
2029

Write Today's Date:_____

Write down an inspirational quote:

My Goals

To-Do List

_____
_____
_____
_____
_____
_____

Art & Letter Fun

Observation Time

Look at the object in the picture.

Do you know what it is?

Yes / No / Unsure

Write down four facts or observations

about the object.

1. _____

2. _____

3. _____

4. _____

Emotions & Moods

How are your feeling today?
Color the facial expressions
to match today's moods.

Can you of three things that might help your mood improve?

1.
2.
3.

Nature Study

Go outside and make a realistic drawing of something you find in in nature.

Reading Time - 1 Hour

Choose Four Books - Read from each book for 15 minutes.

Copy a sentence or picture from each book here:

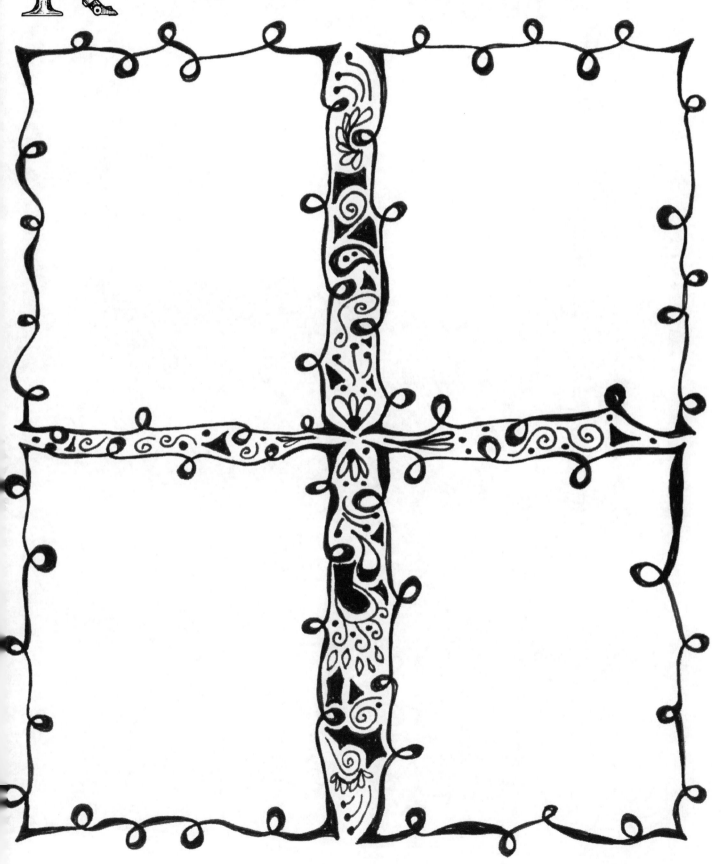

Circle Today's Date

January
February
March
April
May
June
July
August
September
October
November
December

1 2 3 4 5 6
7 8 9 10 11
12 13 14 15
16 17 18 19
20 21 22 23
24 25 26 27
28 29 30 31

MONDAY
TUESDAY
WEDNESDAY
THURSDAY
FRIDAY
SATURDAY
SUNDAY

2015
2016
2017
2018
2019
2020
2021
2022
2023
2024
2025
2026
2027
2028
2029

Write Today's Date:_____

Spelling Time

S

Find 20 Words with **6** letters each.
Look in your books for words.
Write the words here:

_____   _____

_____   _____

_____   _____

_____   _____

_____   _____

_____   _____

_____   _____

_____   _____

_____   _____

Film Study

Watch a Documentary, Educational Program, Movie, or YouTube Tutorial.

TIME:

TITLE:

TOPIC: _____

I learned: _____

_____

_____

_____

NOTES:

Draw a Scene From the Film:

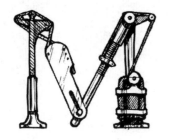

Math Practice

You can design something. You can make graphs, maps, or geometric designs. You can practice math problems.

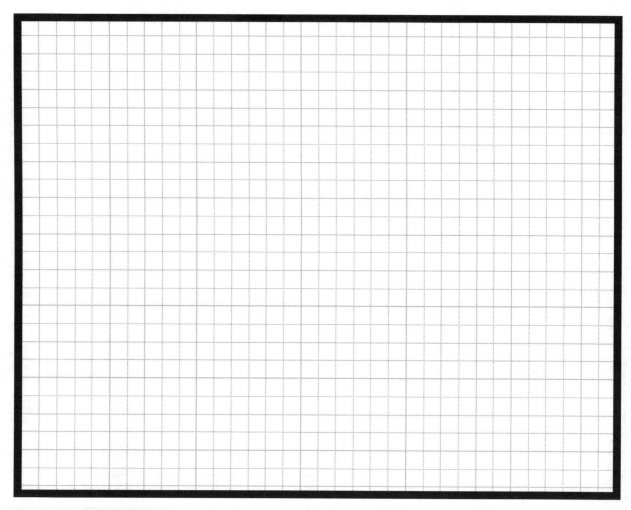

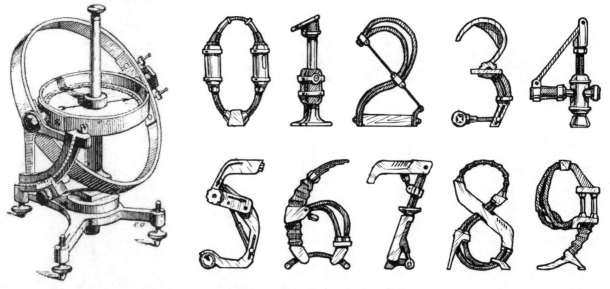

Fun Writing Practice:

ABCDEFGHIJKLMNOPQURSTUVWXYZ

abcdefghijklmnopqrstuvwxyz

ABCDEFGHIJKLMNOPQURSTUVWXYZ

ABCDEFGHIJKLMNOPQURSTUVWXYZ

abcdefghijklmnopqrstuvwxyz

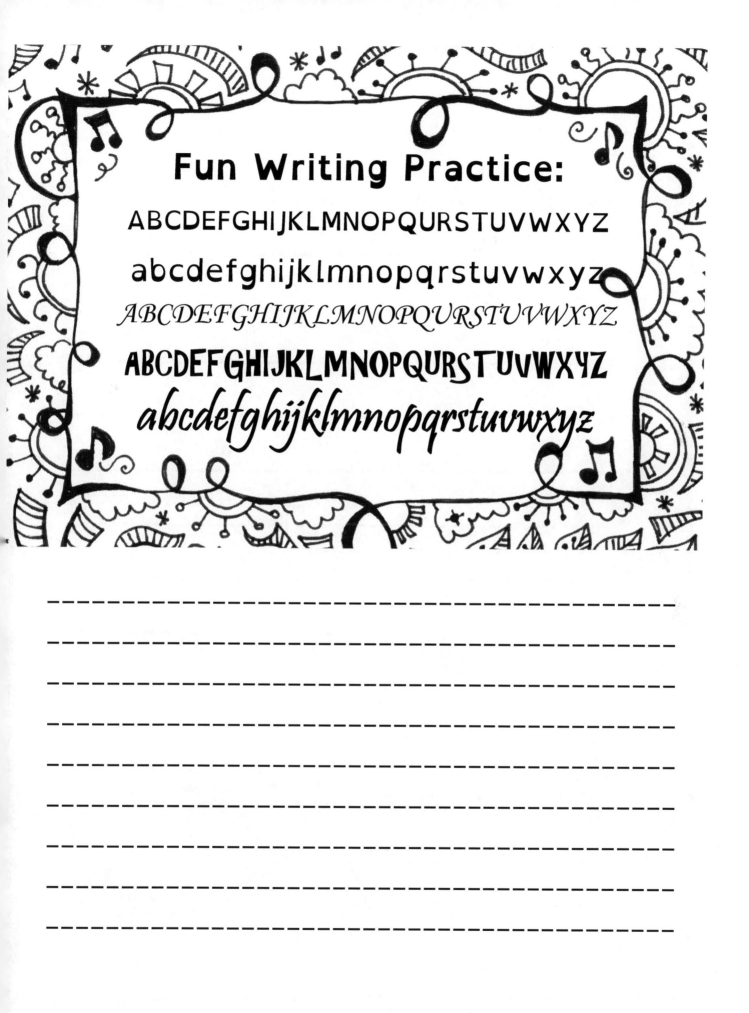

Copywork

Find an interesting paragraph in one of your books and copy it. Be diligent to make your writing look exactly like it does the book.

TITLE:_____

Page Number:_____

_____

_____

_____

_____

_____

_____

_____

_____

_____

Creative
Coloring Time

Circle Today's Date

January
February
March
April
May
June
July
August
September
October
November
December

1 2 3 4 5 6
7 8 9 10 11
12 13 14 15
16 17 18 19
20 21 22 23
24 25 26 27
28 29 30 31

MONDAY
TUESDAY
WEDNESDAY
THURSDAY
FRIDAY
SATURDAY
SUNDAY

2015
2016
2017
2018
2019
2020
2021
2022
2023
2024
2025
2026
2027
2028
2029

Write Today's Date:_____

Write down an inspirational quote:

My Goals

To-Do List

_____
_____
_____
_____
_____
_____

Art & Letter Fun

Observation Time

Look at the object in the picture.

Do you know what it is?

Yes / No / Unsure

Write down four facts or observations
about the object.

1. _____

2. _____

3. _____

4. _____

Emotions & Moods

How are your feeling today?
Color the facial expressions
to match today's moods.

Can you of three things that might help your mood improve?

1.
2.
3.

Nature Study

Go outside and make a realistic
drawing of something you find in
in nature.

Reading Time - 1 Hour

Choose Four Books - Read from each book for 15 minutes.

Copy a sentence or picture from each book here:

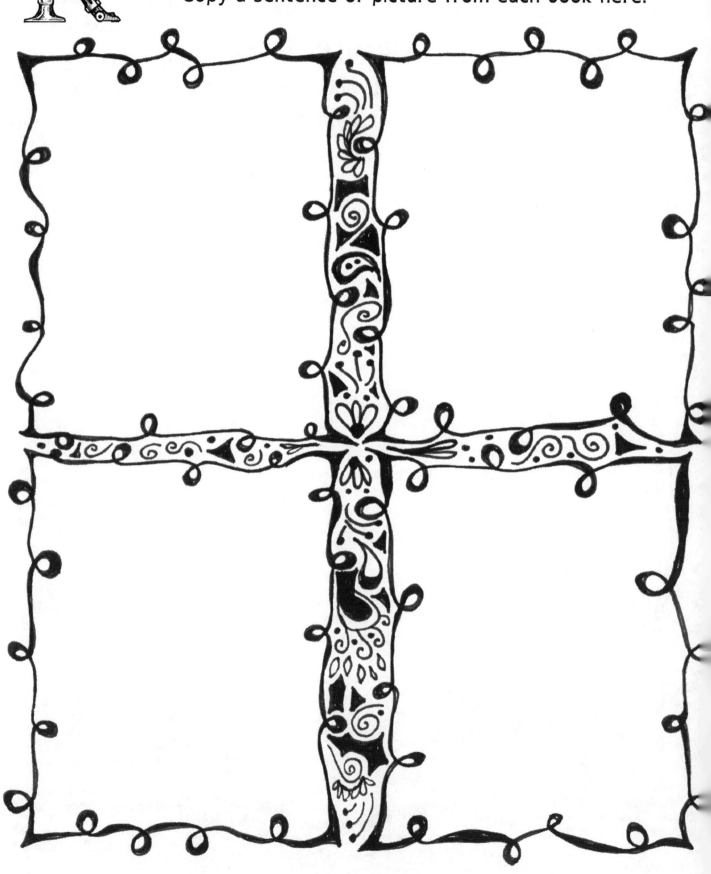

Circle Today's Date

January
February
March
April
May
June
July
August
September
October
November
December

1 2 3 4 5 6
7 8 9 10 11
12 13 14 15
16 17 18 19
20 21 22 23
24 25 26 27
28 29 30 31

MONDAY
TUESDAY
WEDNESDAY
THURSDAY
FRIDAY
SATURDAY
SUNDAY

2015
2016
2017
2018
2019
2020
2021
2022
2023
2024
2025
2026
2027
2028
2029

Write Today's Date: _ _ _ _ _ _ _ _ _ _ _ _ _ _

Spelling Time

Find 20 Words with 7 letters each.

Look in your books for words.

Write the words here:

Film Study

Watch a Documentary, Educational Program, Movie, or YouTube Tutorial.

TIME:

TITLE:

TOPIC: _____

I learned: _____

_____

_____

_____

NOTES:

Draw a Scene From the Film:

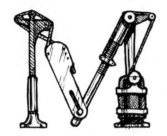

Math Practice

You can design something. You can make graphs, maps, or geometric designs. You can practice math problems.

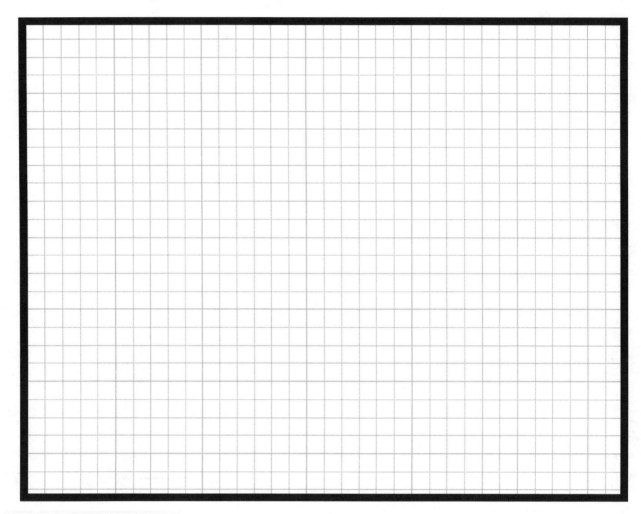

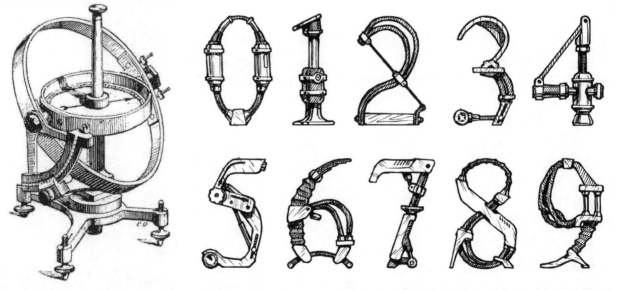

Copywork

Find an interesting paragraph in one of your books and copy it. Be diligent to make your writing look exactly like it does the book.

TITLE:_____

Page Number:_____

_____

_____

_____

_____

_____

_____

_____

_____

_____

Creative
Coloring Time

Circle Today's Date

January
February
March
April
May
June
July
August
September
October
November
December

1 2 3 4 5 6
7 8 9 10 11
12 13 14 15
16 17 18 19
20 21 22 23
24 25 26 27
28 29 30 31

MONDAY
TUESDAY
WEDNESDAY
THURSDAY
FRIDAY
SATURDAY
SUNDAY

2015
2016
2017
2018
2019
2020
2021
2022
2023
2024
2025
2026
2027
2028
2029

Write Today's Date:_____

Art & Letter Fun

Observation Time

Look at the object in the picture.

Do you know what it is?

Yes / No / Unsure

Write down four facts or observations
about the object.

1. _____
2. _____
3. _____
4. _____

Emotions & Moods

How are your feeling today?
Color the facial expressions
to match today's moods.

Can you of three things that might help your mood improve?

1.
2.
3.

Nature Study

Go outside and make a realistic drawing of something you find in in nature.

Reading Time - 1 Hour

Choose Four Books - Read from each book for 15 minutes.

Copy a sentence or picture from each book here:

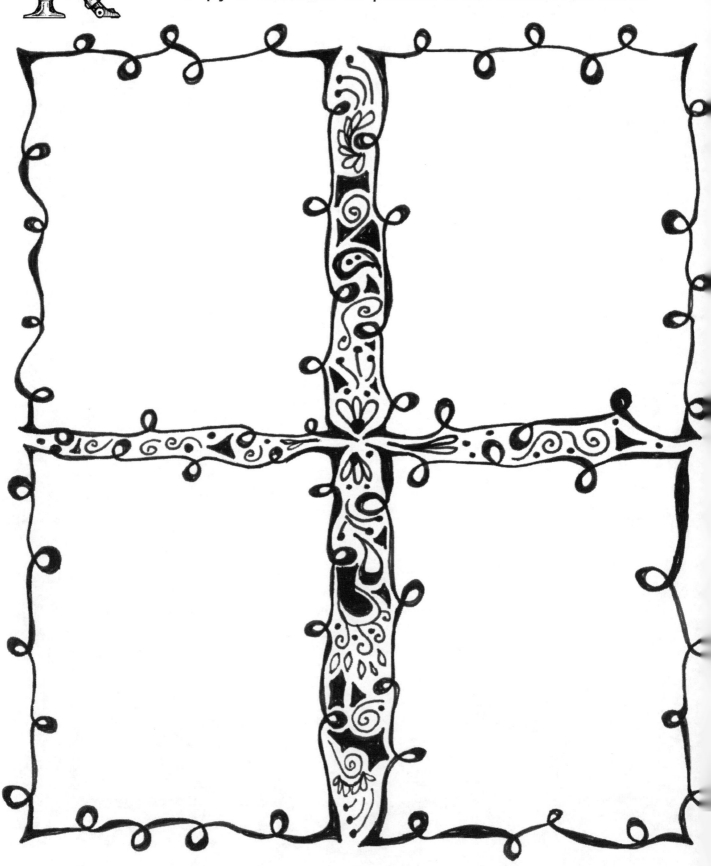

Circle Today's Date

January
February
March
April
May
June
July
August
September
October
November
December

1 2 3 4 5 6
7 8 9 10 11
12 13 14 15
16 17 18 19
20 21 22 23
24 25 26 27
28 29 30 31

MONDAY
TUESDAY
WEDNESDAY
THURSDAY
FRIDAY
SATURDAY
SUNDAY

2015
2016
2017
2018
2019
2020
2021
2022
2023
2024
2025
2026
2027
2028
2029

Write Today's Date: _ _ _ _ _ _ _ _ _ _ _ _ _ _ _ _ _

Spelling Time

Find 20 Words with **8** letters each.

Look in your books for words.

Write the words here:

_____   _____

_____   _____

_____   _____

_____   _____

_____   _____

_____   _____

_____   _____

_____   _____

_____   _____

Film Study

Watch a Documentary, Educational Program, Movie, or YouTube Tutorial.

TIME:

TITLE:

TOPIC: _____

I learned:_____

_____

_____

_____

NOTES:

Draw a Scene From the Film:

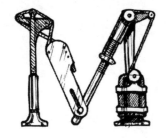

Math Practice

You can design something. You can make graphs, maps, or geometric designs. You can practice math problems.

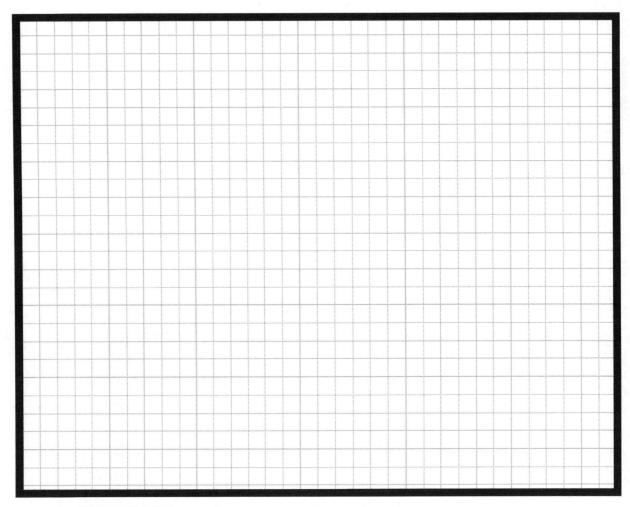

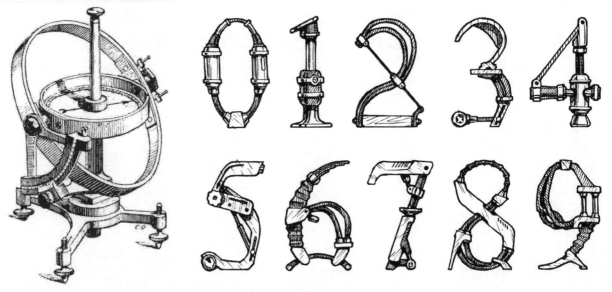

Listening Time

Listen to an audio book or classical music or ask someone to read a story to you while you color and draw on the next page.

What are you listening to?

_____

 Creative
Coloring Time

Circle Today's Date

January
February
March
April
May
June
July
August
September
October
November
December

1 2 3 4 5 6
7 8 9 10 11
12 13 14 15
16 17 18 19
20 21 22 23
24 25 26 27
28 29 30 31

MONDAY
TUESDAY
WEDNESDAY
THURSDAY
FRIDAY
SATURDAY
SUNDAY

2015
2016
2017
2018
2019
2020
2021
2022
2023
2024
2025
2026
2027
2028
2029

Write Today's Date:_____

Write down an inspirational quote:

My Goals

To-Do List

_____

_____

_____

_____

_____

_____

Art & Letter Fun

Observation Time

Look at the object in the picture.

Do you know what it is?

Yes / No / Unsure

Write down four facts or observations

about the object.

1. _____

2. _____

3. _____

4. _____

Emotions & Moods

How are your feeling today?
Color the facial expressions
to match today's moods.

Can you of three things that might help your mood improve?

1.
2.
3.

Nature Study

Go outside and make a realistic
drawing of something you find in
in nature.

Reading Time - 1 Hour

Choose Four Books - Read from each book for 15 minutes.

Copy a sentence or picture from each book here:

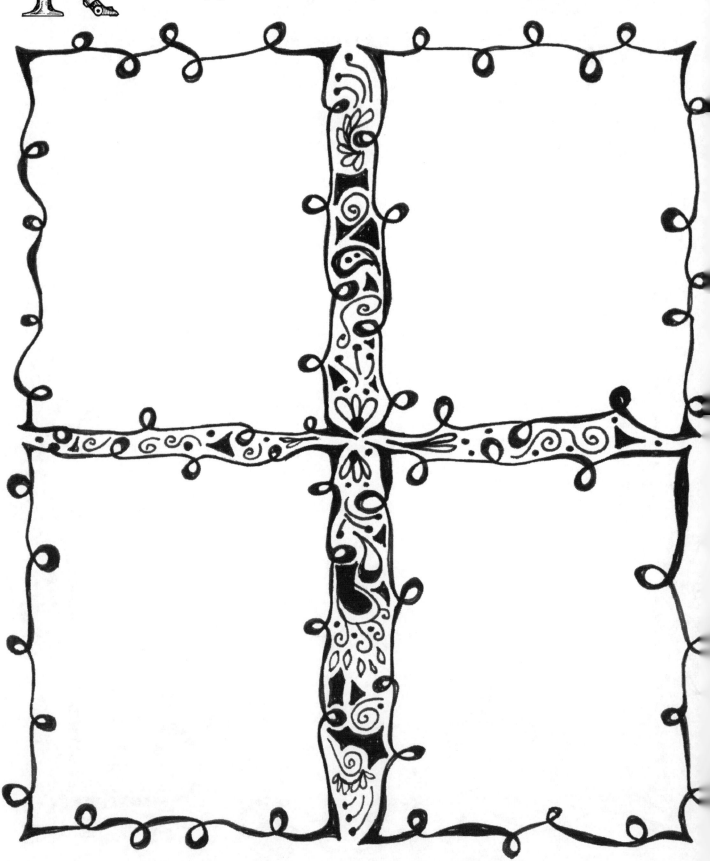

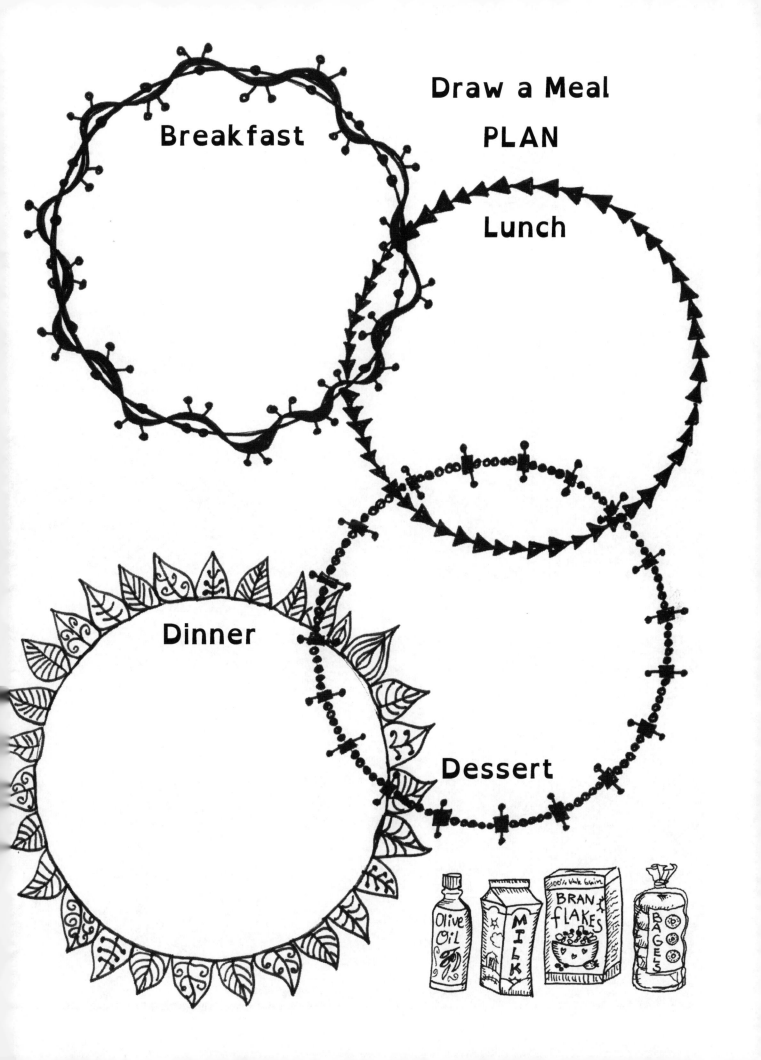

Circle Today's Date

January
February
March
April
May
June
July
August
September
October
November
December

1 2 3 4 5 6
7 8 9 10 11
12 13 14 15
16 17 18 19
20 21 22 23
24 25 26 27
28 29 30 31

MONDAY
TUESDAY
WEDNESDAY
THURSDAY
FRIDAY
SATURDAY
SUNDAY

2015
2016
2017
2018
2019
2020
2021
2022
2023
2024
2025
2026
2027
2028
2029

Write Today's Date:_____

Spelling Time

S

Find 20 Words with **9** letters each.
Look in your books for words.
Write the words here:

_____   _____

_____   _____

_____   _____

_____   _____

_____   _____

_____   _____

_____   _____

_____   _____

_____   _____

_____   _____

Film Study

Watch a Documentary, Educational Program, Movie, or YouTube Tutorial.

TIME:

TITLE:

TOPIC: _____

I learned:_____

_____

_____

_____

NOTES:

Draw a Scene From the Film:

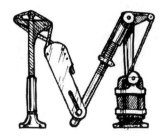

Math Practice

You can design something. You can make graphs, maps, or geometric designs. You can practice math problems.

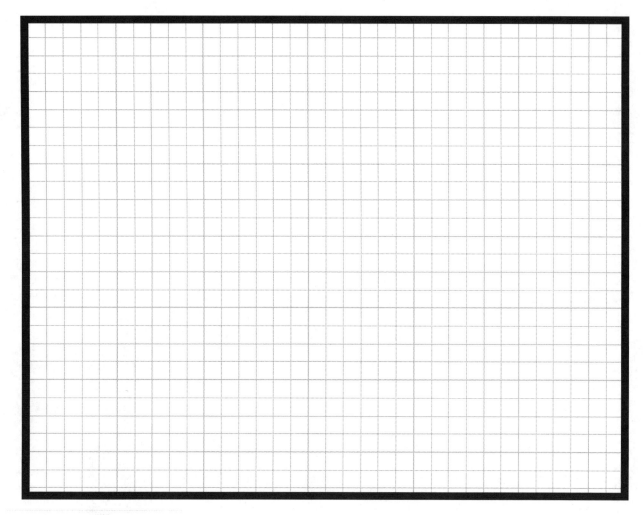

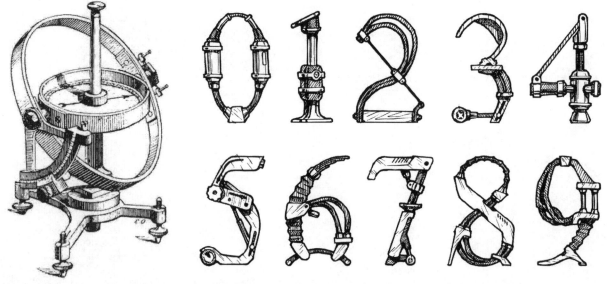

World News Today!

Talk to your parents about current events.

Look at a newspaper, news broadcast or website.

Color the countries your learn about.

Tell the news stories with words or pictures.

Copywork

Find an interesting paragraph in one of your books and copy it. Be diligent to make your writing look exactly like it does the book.

TITLE:_____

Page Number:_____

_____

_____

_____

_____

_____

_____

_____

_____

_____

Creative
Coloring Time

Circle Today's Date

January
February
March
April
May
June
July
August
September
October
November
December

1 2 3 4 5 6
7 8 9 10 11
12 13 14 15
16 17 18 19
20 21 22 23
24 25 26 27
28 29 30 31

MONDAY
TUESDAY
WEDNESDAY
THURSDAY
FRIDAY
SATURDAY
SUNDAY

2015
2016
2017
2018
2019
2020
2021
2022
2023
2024
2025
2026
2027
2028
2029

Write Today's Date:_____

Write down an inspirational quote:

My Goals

To-Do List

_____
_____
_____
_____
_____
_____

Art & Letter Fun

Observation Time

Look at the object in the picture.

Do you know what it is?

Yes / No / Unsure

Write down four facts or observations

1. _____

2. _____

3. _____

4. _____

Emotions & Moods

How are your feeling today?
Color the facial expressions
to match today's moods.

Can you of three things that might help your mood improve?

1.
2.
3.

Nature Study

Go outside and make a realistic
drawing of something you find in
in nature.

Reading Time - 1 Hour

Choose Four Books - Read from each book for 15 minutes.

Copy a sentence or picture from each book here:

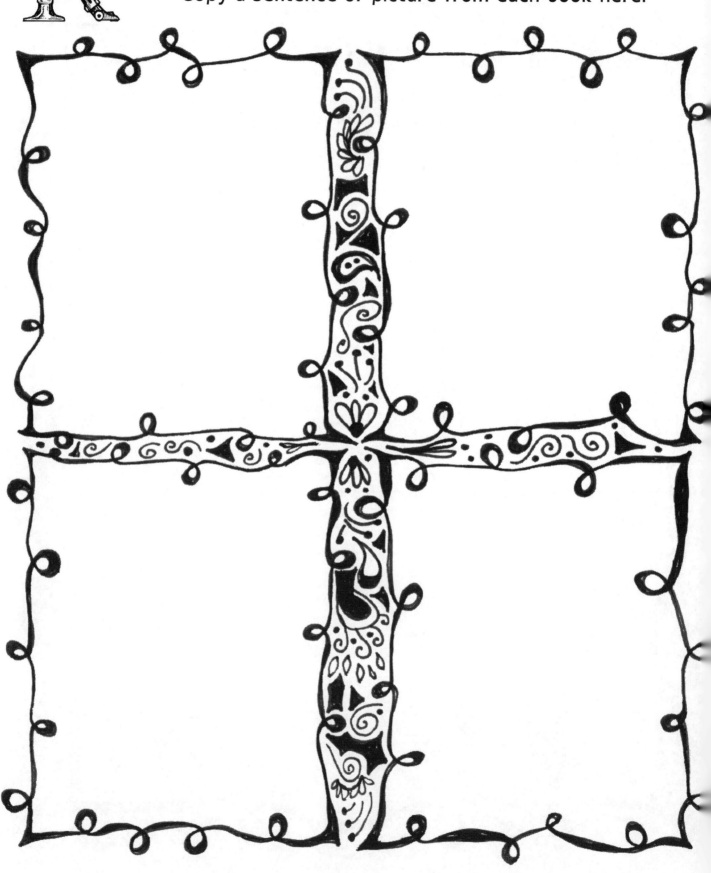

Circle Today's Date

January
February
March
April
May
June
July
August
September
October
November
December

1 2 3 4 5 6
7 8 9 10 11
12 13 14 15
16 17 18 19
20 21 22 23
24 25 26 27
28 29 30 31

MONDAY
TUESDAY
WEDNESDAY
THURSDAY
FRIDAY
SATURDAY
SUNDAY

2015
2016
2017
2018
2019
2020
2021
2022
2023
2024
2025
2026
2027
2028
2029

Write Today's Date:_____

Spelling Time

Find 20 Words with **8** letters each.
Look in your books for words.
Write the words here:

_____   _____

_____   _____

_____   _____

_____   _____

_____   _____

_____   _____

_____   _____

_____   _____

_____   _____

_____   _____

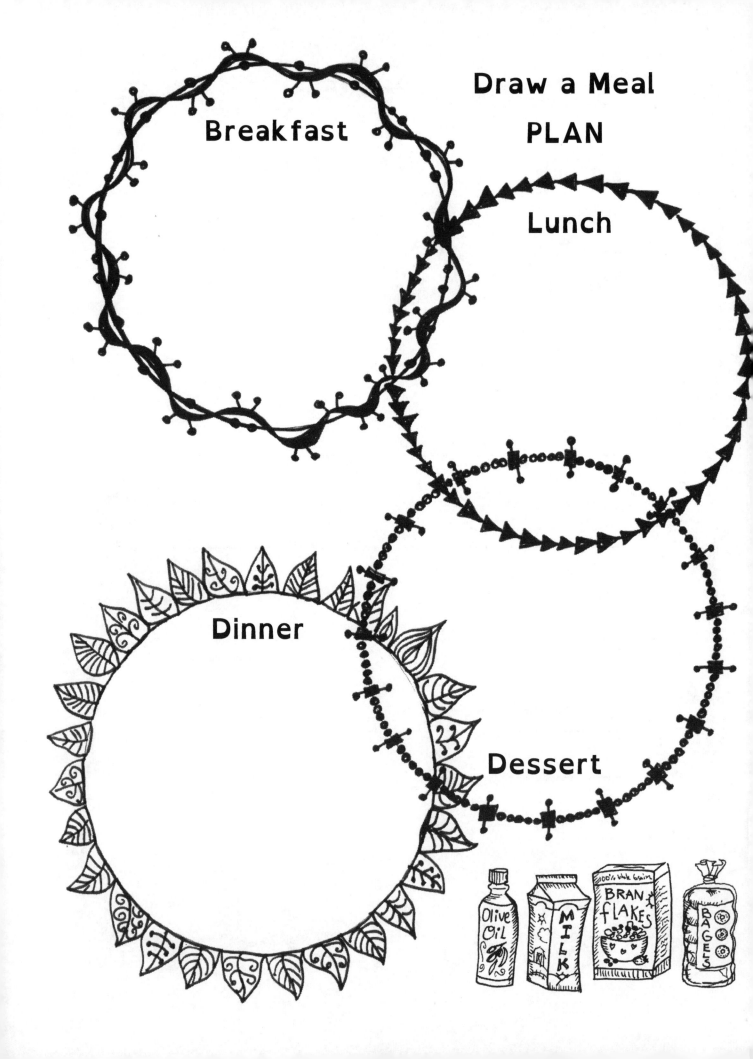

Film Study

Watch a Documentary, Educational
Program, Movie, or YouTube Tutorial.

TIME:

TITLE:

TOPIC: _____

I learned:_____

_____

_____

_____

NOTES:

Draw a Scene From the Film:

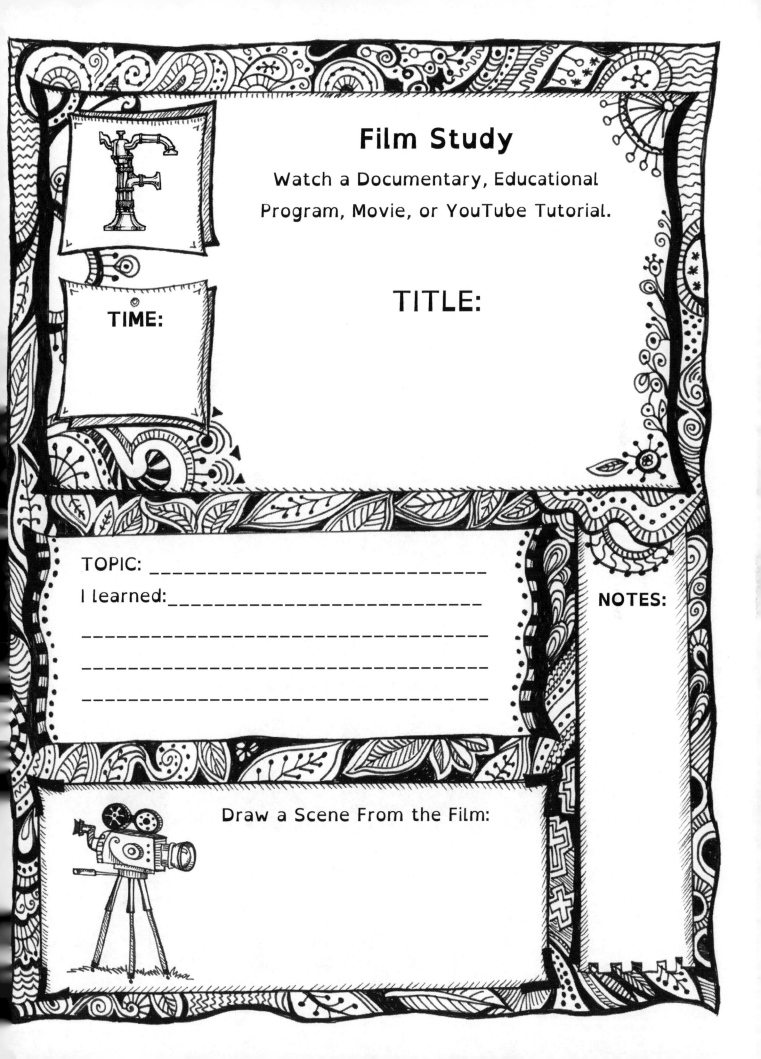

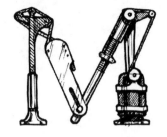

Math Practice

You can design something. You can make graphs, maps, or geometric designs. You can practice math problems.

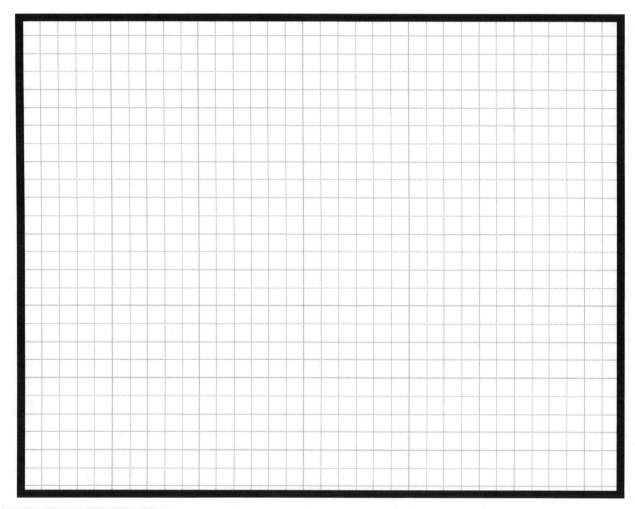

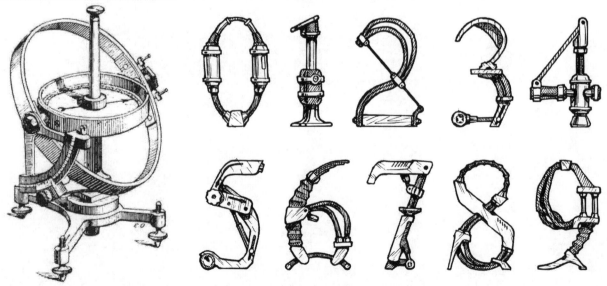

Fun Writing Practice:

ABCDEFGHIJKLMNOPQURSTUVWXYZ

abcdefghijklmnopqrstuvwxyz

ABCDEFGHIJKLMNOPQURSTUVWXYZ

ABCDEFGHIJKLMNOPQURSTUVWXYZ

abcdefghijklmnopqrstuvwxyz

Copywork

Find an interesting paragraph in one of your books and copy it. Be diligent to make your writing look exactly like it does the book.

TITLE:_____

Page Number:_____

_____

_____

_____

_____

_____

_____

_____

_____

_____

Creative
Coloring Time

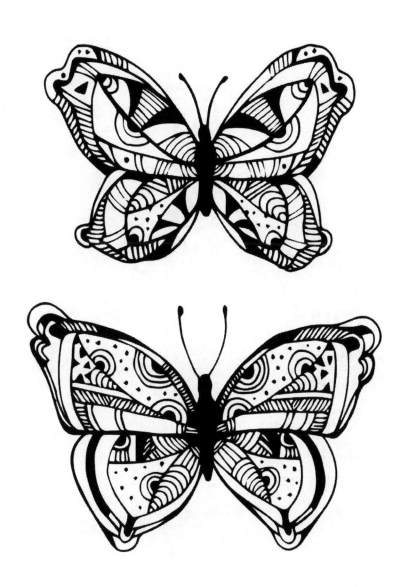

Circle Today's Date

January
February
March
April
May
June
July
August
September
October
November
December

1 2 3 4 5 6
7 8 9 10 11
12 13 14 15
16 17 18 19
20 21 22 23
24 25 26 27
28 29 30 31

MONDAY
TUESDAY
WEDNESDAY
THURSDAY
FRIDAY
SATURDAY
SUNDAY

2015
2016
2017
2018
2019
2020
2021
2022
2023
2024
2025
2026
2027
2028
2029

Write Today's Date: _ _ _ _ _ _ _ _ _ _ _ _ _ _

Write down an inspirational quote:

My Goals

To-Do List

_____
_____
_____
_____
_____
_____

Art & Letter Fun

Observation Time

Look at the object in the picture.

Do you know what it is?

Yes / No / Unsure

Write down four facts or observations

about the object.

1. _____

2. _____

3. _____

4. _____

Emotions & Moods

How are your feeling today?
Color the facial expressions
to match today's moods.

Can you of three things that might help your mood improve?

1.
2.
3.

Nature Study

Go outside and make a realistic
drawing of something you find in
in nature.

Reading Time - 1 Hour

Choose Four Books - Read from each book for 15 minutes.

Copy a sentence or picture from each book here:

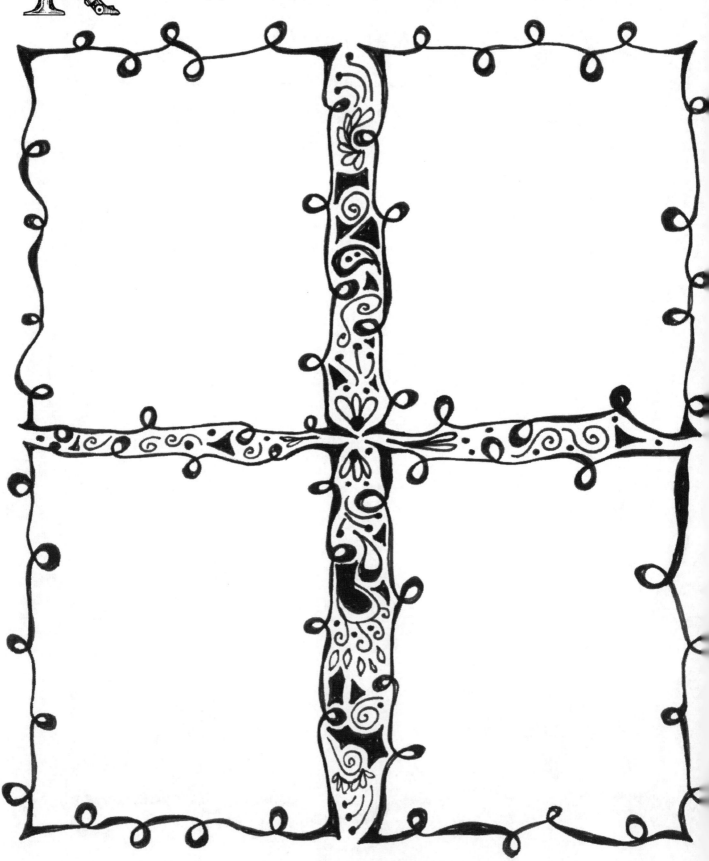

Circle Today's Date

January
February
March
April
May
June
July
August
September
October
November
December

1 2 3 4 5 6
7 8 9 10 11
12 13 14 15
16 17 18 19
20 21 22 23
24 25 26 27
28 29 30 31

MONDAY
TUESDAY
WEDNESDAY
THURSDAY
FRIDAY
SATURDAY
SUNDAY

2015
2016
2017
2018
2019
2020
2021
2022
2023
2024
2025
2026
2027
2028
2029

Write Today's Date:_____

Spelling Time

S

Find 20 Words with **7** letters each.
Look in your books for words.
Write the words here:

_____   _____

_____   _____

_____   _____

_____   _____

_____   _____

_____   _____

_____   _____

_____   _____

_____   _____

_____   _____

Film Study

Watch a Documentary, Educational Program, Movie, or YouTube Tutorial.

TITLE:

TIME:

TOPIC: _____

I learned: _____

_____

_____

_____

NOTES:

Draw a Scene From the Film:

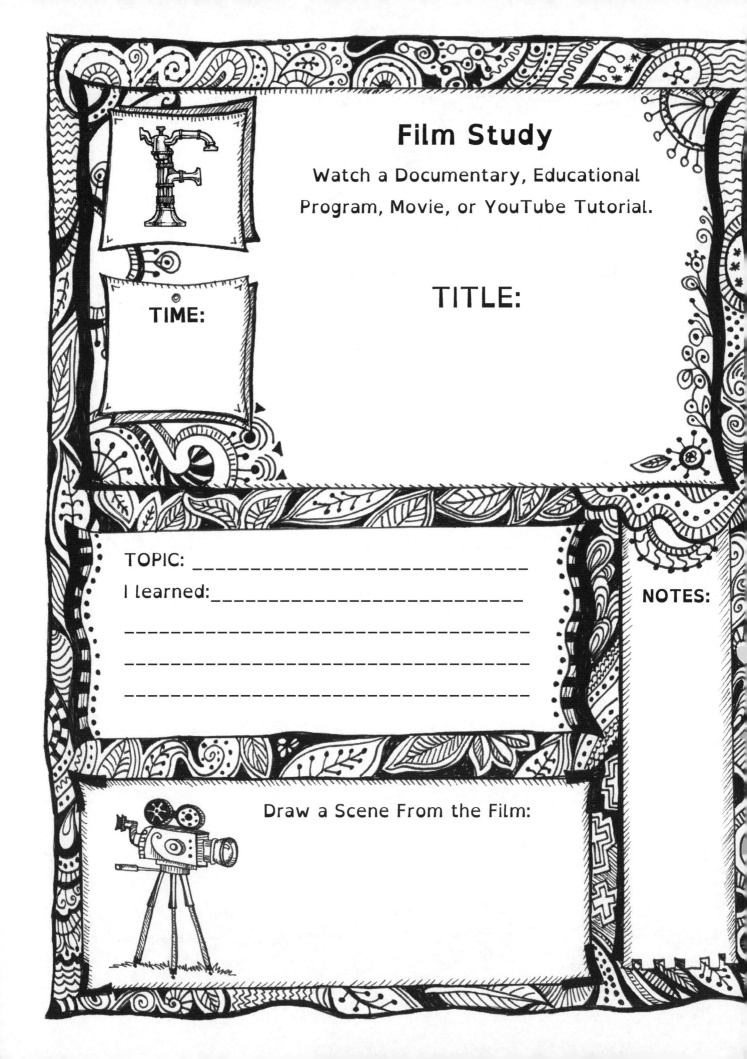

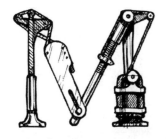

Math Practice

You can design something. You can make
graphs, maps, or geometric designs.
You can practice math problems.

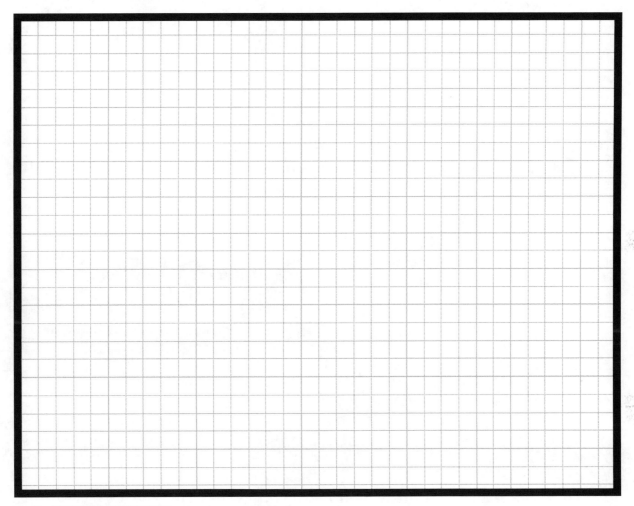

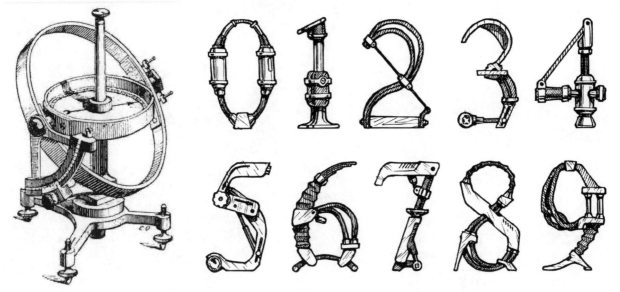

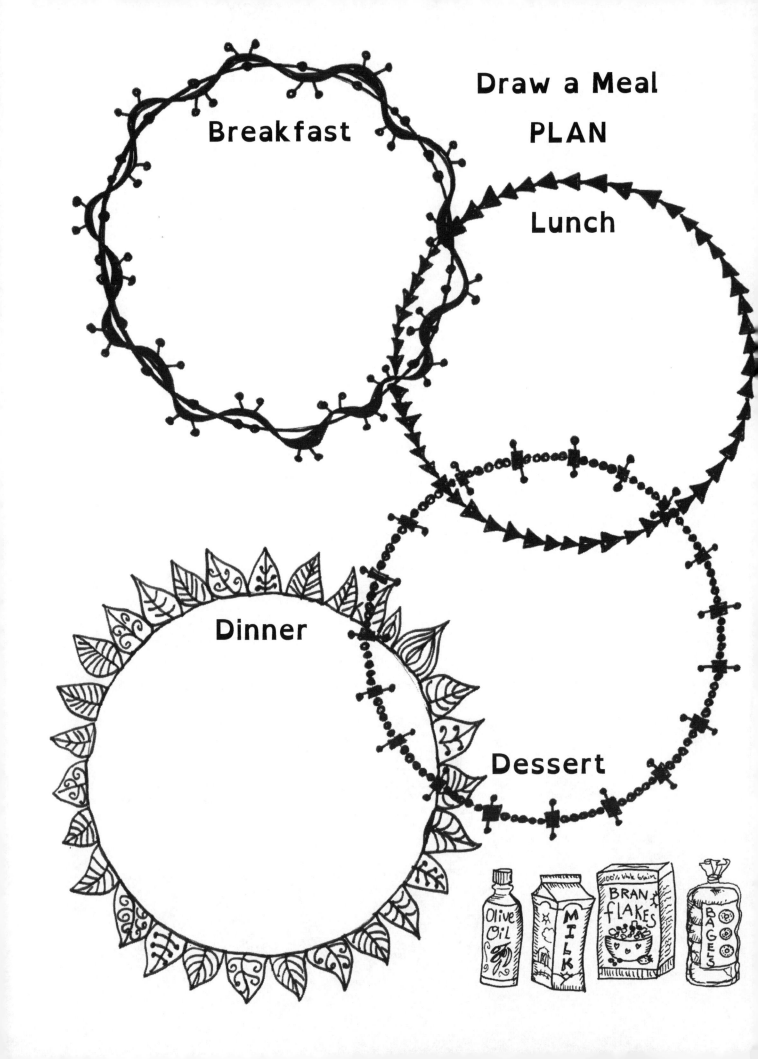

Breakfast

Draw a Meal
PLAN

Lunch

Dinner

Dessert

Copywork

Find an interesting paragraph in one of your books and copy it. Be diligent to make your writing look exactly like it does the book.

TITLE:_____

Page Number:_____

_____

_____

_____

_____

_____

_____

_____

_____

_____

Creative
Coloring Time

Circle Today's Date

January
February
March
April
May
June
July
August
September
October
November
December

1 2 3 4 5 6
7 8 9 10 11
12 13 14 15
16 17 18 19
20 21 22 23
24 25 26 27
28 29 30 31

MONDAY
TUESDAY
WEDNESDAY
THURSDAY
FRIDAY
SATURDAY
SUNDAY

2015
2016
2017
2018
2019
2020
2021
2022
2023
2024
2025
2026
2027
2028
2029

Write Today's Date: _ _ _ _ _ _ _ _ _ _ _ _ _ _ _

Write down an inspirational quote:

My Goals

To-Do List

_____
_____
_____
_____
_____
_____

Art & Letter Fun

Observation Time

Look at the object in the picture.

Do you know what it is?

Yes / No / Unsure

Write down four facts or observations

about the object.

1. _____

2. _____

3. _____

4. _____

Emotions & Moods

How are your feeling today?
Color the facial expressions
to match today's moods.

Can you of three things that might help your mood improve?

1.
2.
3.

Nature Study

Go outside and make a realistic drawing of something you find in in nature.

Reading Time - 1 Hour

Choose Four Books - Read from each book for 15 minutes.

Copy a sentence or picture from each book here:

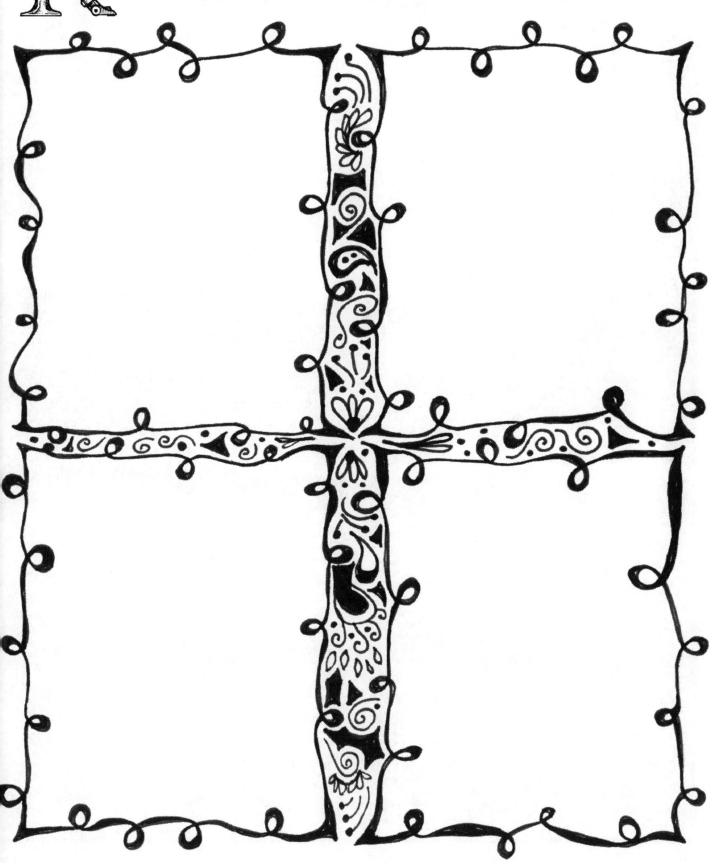

Circle Today's Date

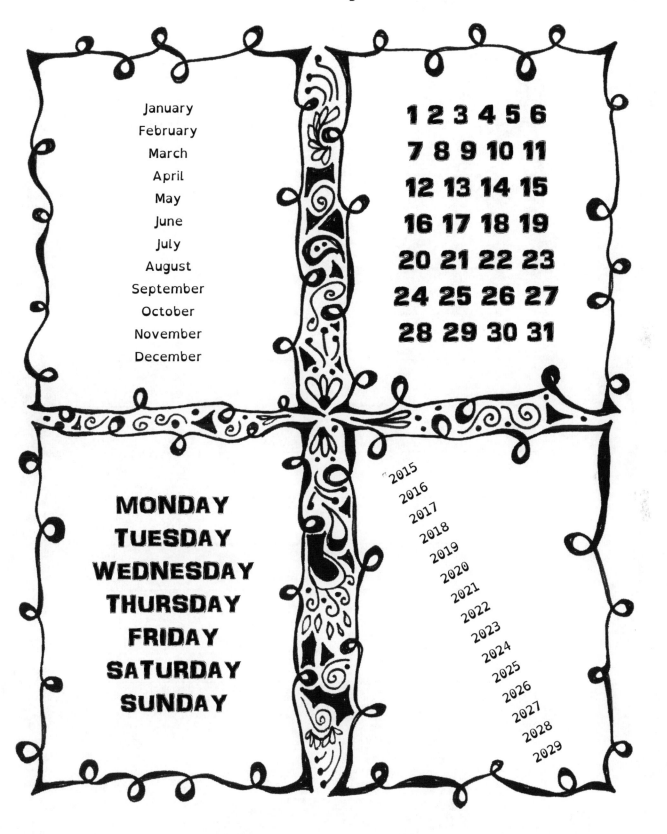

January
February
March
April
May
June
July
August
September
October
November
December

1 2 3 4 5 6
7 8 9 10 11
12 13 14 15
16 17 18 19
20 21 22 23
24 25 26 27
28 29 30 31

MONDAY
TUESDAY
WEDNESDAY
THURSDAY
FRIDAY
SATURDAY
SUNDAY

2015
2016
2017
2018
2019
2020
2021
2022
2023
2024
2025
2026
2027
2028
2029

Write Today's Date: _ _ _ _ _ _ _ _ _ _ _ _ _ _ _ _ _

Spelling Time

Find 20 Words with **6** letters each.
Look in your books for words.
Write the words here:

Film Study

Watch a Documentary, Educational Program, Movie, or YouTube Tutorial.

TIME:

TITLE:

TOPIC: _____

I learned:_____

_____

_____

_____

NOTES:

Draw a Scene From the Film:

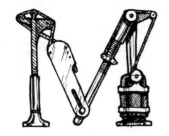

Math Practice

You can design something. You can make
graphs, maps, or geometric designs.
You can practice math problems.

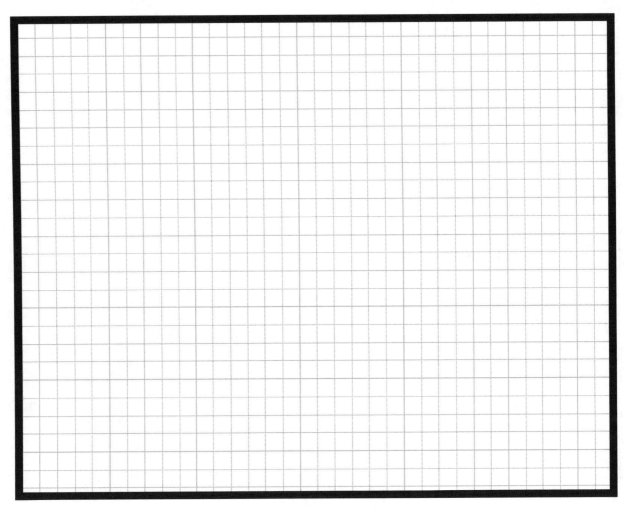

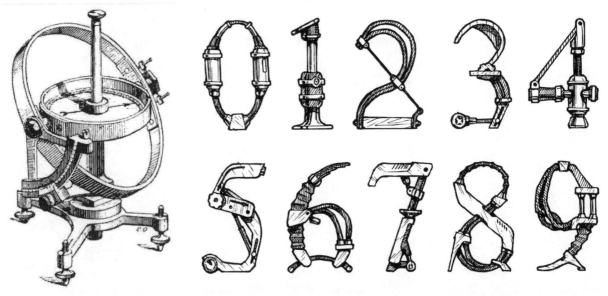

Copywork

Find an interesting paragraph in one of your books and copy it. Be diligent to make your writing look exactly like it does the book.

TITLE:_____

Page Number:_____

_____

_____

_____

_____

_____

_____

_____

_____

_____

_____

Creative
Coloring Time

Circle Today's Date

January
February
March
April
May
June
July
August
September
October
November
December

1 2 3 4 5 6
7 8 9 10 11
12 13 14 15
16 17 18 19
20 21 22 23
24 25 26 27
28 29 30 31

MONDAY
TUESDAY
WEDNESDAY
THURSDAY
FRIDAY
SATURDAY
SUNDAY

2015
2016
2017
2018
2019
2020
2021
2022
2023
2024
2025
2026
2027
2028
2029

Write Today's Date:_____

Write down an inspirational quote:

My Goals

To-Do List

_____
_____
_____
_____
_____
_____

Art & Letter Fun

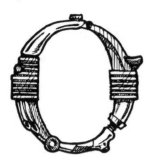

Observation Time

Look at the object in the picture.

Do you know what it is?

Yes / No / Unsure

Write down four facts or observations

about the object.

1. _____

2. _____

3. _____

4. _____

Emotions & Moods

How are your feeling today?
Color the facial expressions
to match today's moods.

Can you of three things that might help your mood improve?

1.
2.
3.

Nature Study

Go outside and make a realistic drawing of something you find in in nature.

Reading Time - 1 Hour

Choose Four Books - Read from each book for 15 minutes.

Copy a sentence or picture from each book here:

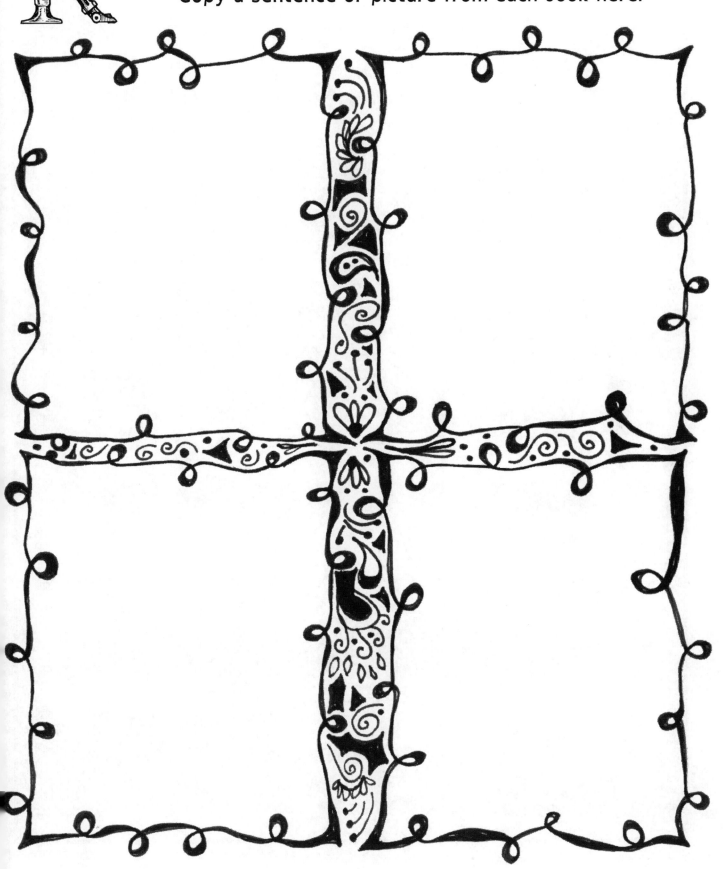

Circle Today's Date

January
February
March
April
May
June
July
August
September
October
November
December

1 2 3 4 5 6
7 8 9 10 11
12 13 14 15
16 17 18 19
20 21 22 23
24 25 26 27
28 29 30 31

MONDAY
TUESDAY
WEDNESDAY
THURSDAY
FRIDAY
SATURDAY
SUNDAY

2015
2016
2017
2018
2019
2020
2021
2022
2023
2024
2025
2026
2027
2028
2029

Write Today's Date: _ _ _ _ _ _ _ _ _ _ _ _

Spelling Time

Find 20 Words with 5 letters each.
Look in your books for words.
Write the words here:

Film Study

Watch a Documentary, Educational Program, Movie, or YouTube Tutorial.

TIME:

TITLE:

TOPIC: _____

I learned: _____

_____

_____

_____

NOTES:

Draw a Scene From the Film:

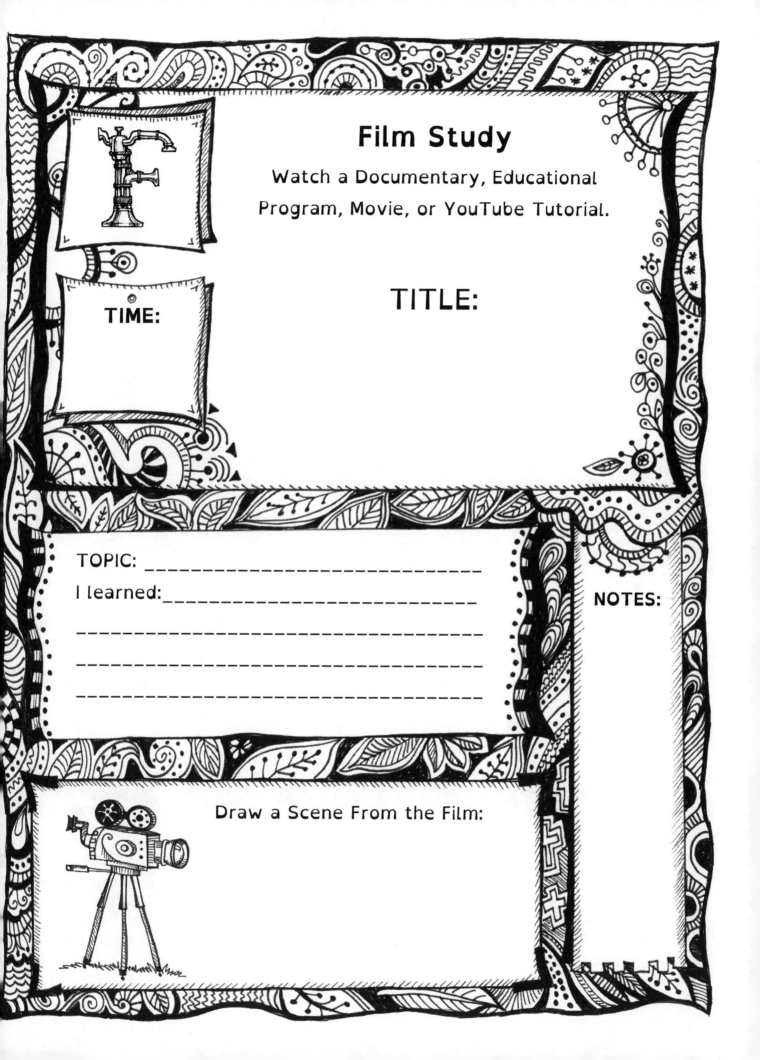

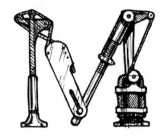

Math Practice

You can design something. You can make graphs, maps, or geometric designs. You can practice math problems.

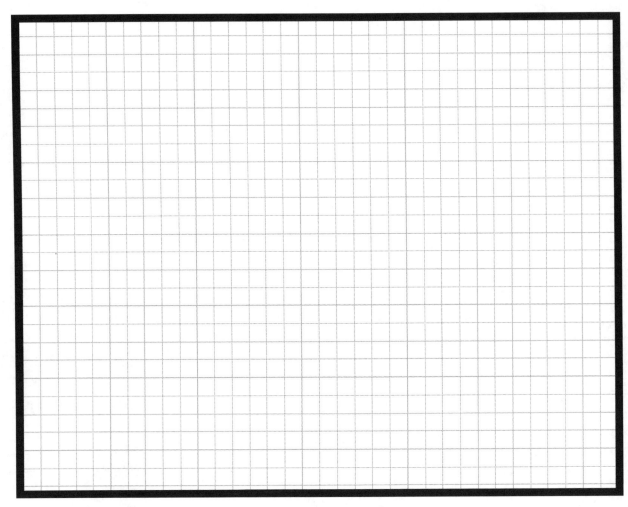

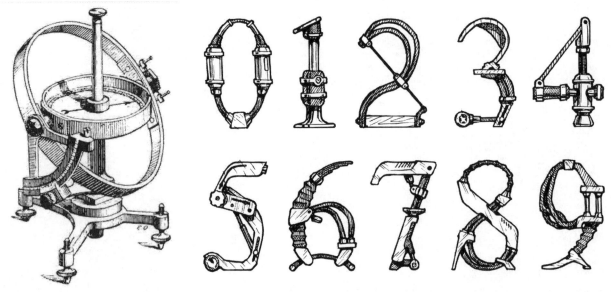

World News Today!

Talk to your parents about current events.

Look at a newspaper, news broadcast or website.

Color the countries your learn about.

Tell the news stories with words or pictures.

Copywork

Find an interesting paragraph in one of your books and copy it. Be diligent to make your writing look exactly like it does the book.

TITLE:_____

Page Number:_____

_____

_____

_____

_____

_____

_____

_____

_____

_____

Creative
Coloring Time

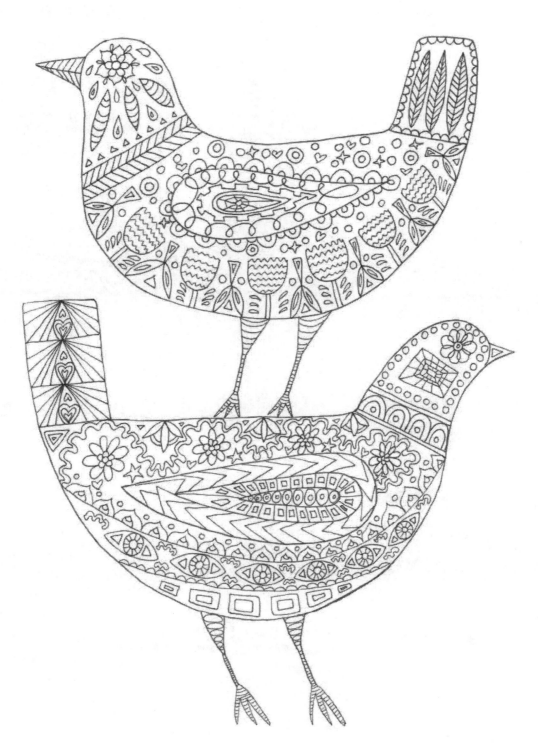

Circle Today's Date

January
February
March
April
May
June
July
August
September
October
November
December

1 2 3 4 5 6
7 8 9 10 11
12 13 14 15
16 17 18 19
20 21 22 23
24 25 26 27
28 29 30 31

MONDAY
TUESDAY
WEDNESDAY
THURSDAY
FRIDAY
SATURDAY
SUNDAY

2015
2016
2017
2018
2019
2020
2021
2022
2023
2024
2025
2026
2027
2028
2029

Write Today's Date:_____

Write down an inspirational quote:

My Goals

To-Do List

_____
_____
_____
_____
_____
_____

Art & Letter Fun

Observation Time

Look at the object in the picture.

Do you know what it is?

Yes / No / Unsure

Write down four facts or observations
about the object.

1. _____

2. _____

3. _____

4. _____

Emotions & Moods

How are your feeling today?
Color the facial expressions
to match today's moods.

Can you of three things that might help your mood improve?

1.

2.

3.

Nature Study

Go outside and make a realistic
drawing of something you find in
in nature.

Reading Time - 1 Hour

Choose Four Books - Read from each book for 15 minutes.

Copy a sentence or picture from each book here:

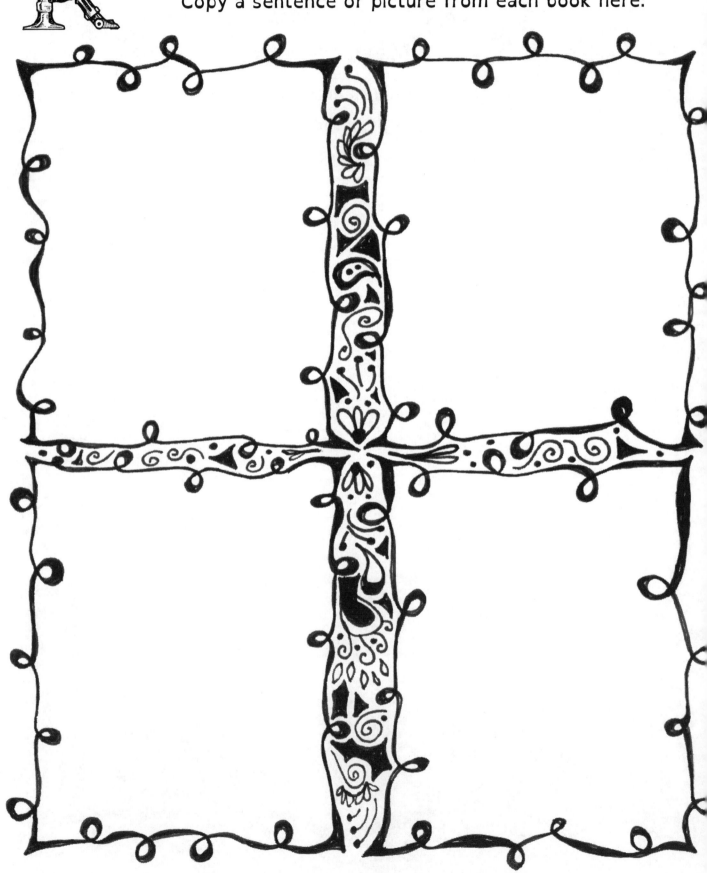

Circle Today's Date

January
February
March
April
May
June
July
August
September
October
November
December

1 2 3 4 5 6
7 8 9 10 11
12 13 14 15
16 17 18 19
20 21 22 23
24 25 26 27
28 29 30 31

MONDAY
TUESDAY
WEDNESDAY
THURSDAY
FRIDAY
SATURDAY
SUNDAY

2015
2016
2017
2018
2019
2020
2021
2022
2023
2024
2025
2026
2027
2028
2029

Write Today's Date:_ _ _ _ _ _ _ _ _ _ _ _ _

Spelling Time

Find 20 Words with 5 letters each.
Look in your books for words.
Write the words here:

_____   _____

_____   _____

_____   _____

_____   _____

_____   _____

_____   _____

_____   _____

_____   _____

_____   _____

Film Study

Watch a Documentary, Educational Program, Movie, or YouTube Tutorial.

TIME:

TITLE:

TOPIC: _____

I learned:_____

_____

_____

_____

NOTES:

Draw a Scene From the Film:

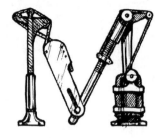

Math Practice

You can design something. You can make graphs, maps, or geometric designs. You can practice math problems.

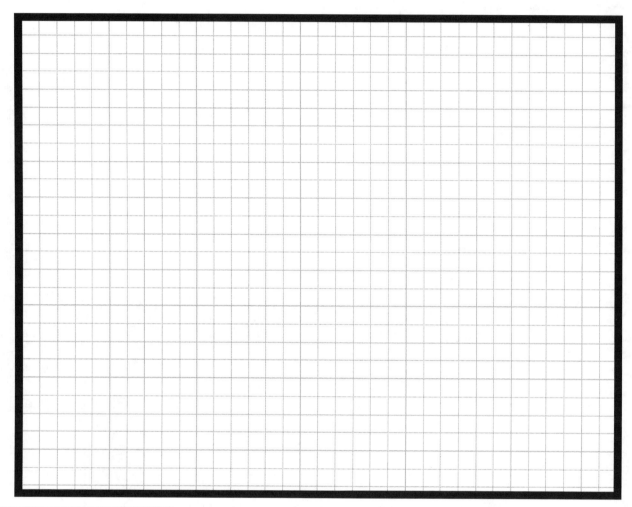

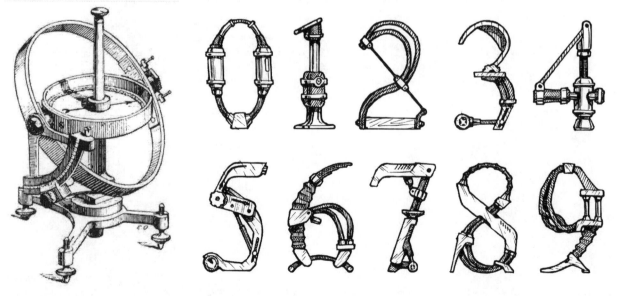

Fun Writing Practice:

ABCDEFGHIJKLMNOPQURSTUVWXYZ

abcdefghijklmnopqrstuvwxyz

ABCDEFGHIJKLMNOPQURSTUVWXYZ

ABCDEFGHIJKLMNOPQURSTUVWXYZ

abcdefghijklmnopqrstuvwxyz

Copywork

Find an interesting paragraph in one of your books and copy it. Be diligent to make your writing look exactly like it does the book.

TITLE:_____

Page Number:_____

_____

_____

_____

_____

_____

_____

_____

_____

_____

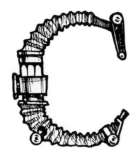

Creative
Coloring Time

Circle Today's Date

January
February
March
April
May
June
July
August
September
October
November
December

1 2 3 4 5 6
7 8 9 10 11
12 13 14 15
16 17 18 19
20 21 22 23
24 25 26 27
28 29 30 31

MONDAY
TUESDAY
WEDNESDAY
THURSDAY
FRIDAY
SATURDAY
SUNDAY

2015
2016
2017
2018
2019
2020
2021
2022
2023
2024
2025
2026
2027
2028
2029

Write Today's Date: _ _ _ _ _ _ _ _ _ _ _ _ _ _ _ _

Write down an inspirational quote:

My Goals

To-Do List

_____
_____
_____
_____
_____
_____

Art & Letter Fun

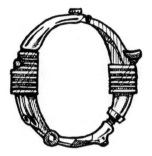

Observation Time

Look at the object in the picture.
Do you know what it is?
Yes / No / Unsure
Write down four facts or observations
about the object.

1. _____

2. _____

3. _____

4. _____

Emotions & Moods

How are your feeling today?
Color the facial expressions
to match today's moods.

Can you of three things that might help your mood improve?

1.
2.
3.

Nature Study

Go outside and make a realistic drawing of something you find in in nature.

Reading Time - 1 Hour

Choose Four Books - Read from each book for 15 minutes.

Copy a sentence or picture from each book here:

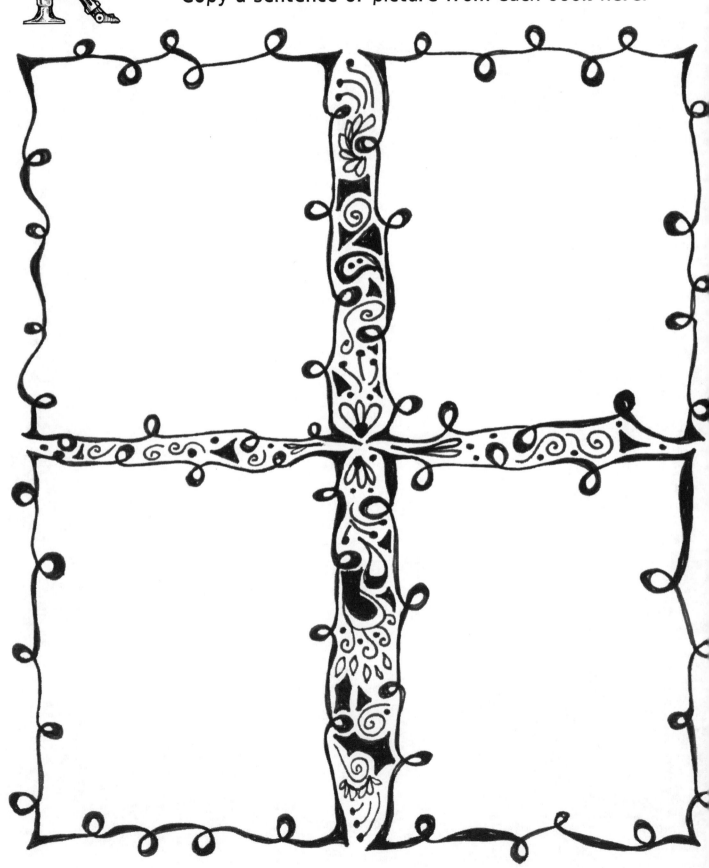

Circle Today's Date

January
February
March
April
May
June
July
August
September
October
November
December

1 2 3 4 5 6
7 8 9 10 11
12 13 14 15
16 17 18 19
20 21 22 23
24 25 26 27
28 29 30 31

MONDAY
TUESDAY
WEDNESDAY
THURSDAY
FRIDAY
SATURDAY
SUNDAY

2015
2016
2017
2018
2019
2020
2021
2022
2023
2024
2025
2026
2027
2028
2029

Write Today's Date: _____

Spelling Time

S

Find **20** Words with **4** letters each.
Look in your books for words.
Write the words here:

_____   _____

_____   _____

_____   _____

_____   _____

_____   _____

_____   _____

_____   _____

_____   _____

_____   _____

Film Study

Watch a Documentary, Educational Program, Movie, or YouTube Tutorial.

TIME:

TITLE:

TOPIC: _____

I learned:_____

_____

_____

_____

NOTES:

Draw a Scene From the Film:

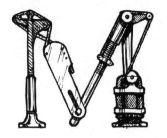

Math Practice

You can design something. You can make
graphs, maps, or geometric designs.
You can practice math problems.

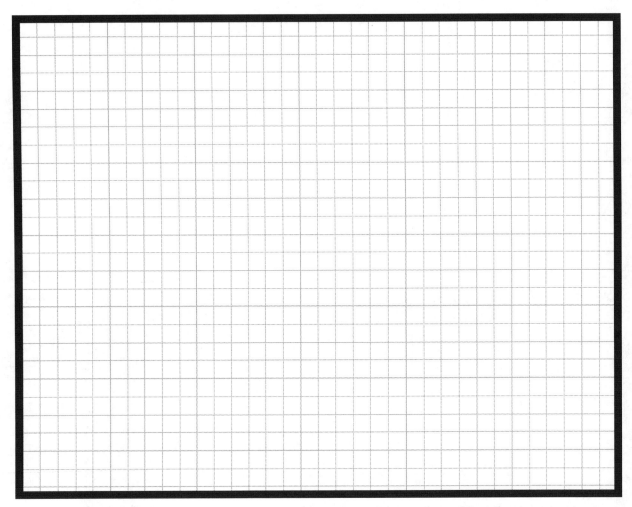

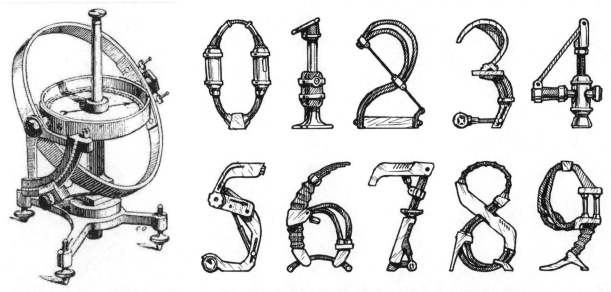

Listening Time

Listen to an audio book or classical music or
ask someone to read a story to you while
you color and draw on the next page.

What are you listening to?

_____

Creative
Coloring Time

Circle Today's Date

January
February
March
April
May
June
July
August
September
October
November
December

1 2 3 4 5 6
7 8 9 10 11
12 13 14 15
16 17 18 19
20 21 22 23
24 25 26 27
28 29 30 31

MONDAY
TUESDAY
WEDNESDAY
THURSDAY
FRIDAY
SATURDAY
SUNDAY

2015
2016
2017
2018
2019
2020
2021
2022
2023
2024
2025
2026
2027
2028
2029

Write Today's Date: _ _ _ _ _ _ _ _ _ _ _ _ _ _

Write down an inspirational quote:

My Goals

To-Do List

_____

_____

_____

_____

_____

_____

Art & Letter Fun

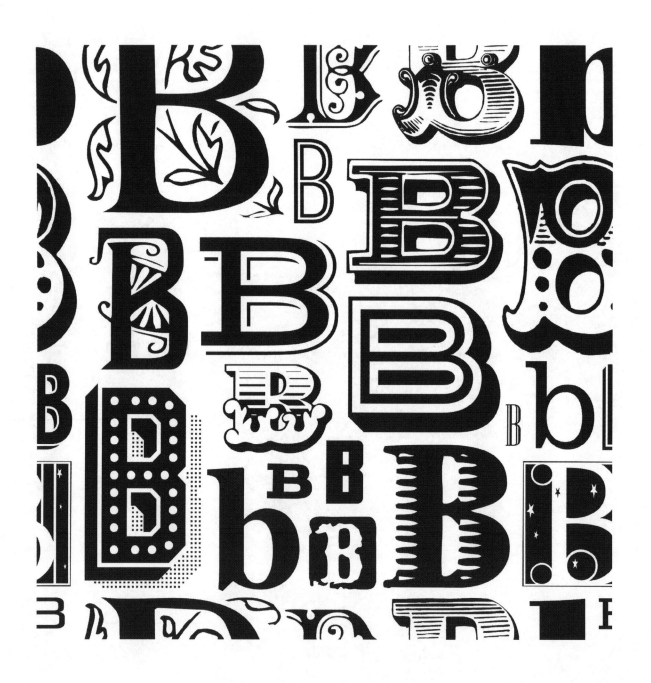

Observation Time

Look at the object in the picture.

Do you know what it is?

Yes / No / Unsure

Write down four facts or observations

about the object.

1. _____

2. _____

3. _____

4. _____

Emotions & Moods

How are your feeling today?
Color the facial expressions
to match today's moods.

Can you of three things that might help your mood improve?

1.
2.
3.

Nature Study

Go outside and make a realistic drawing of something you find in in nature.

Reading Time - 1 Hour

Choose Four Books - Read from each book for 15 minutes.

Copy a sentence or picture from each book here:

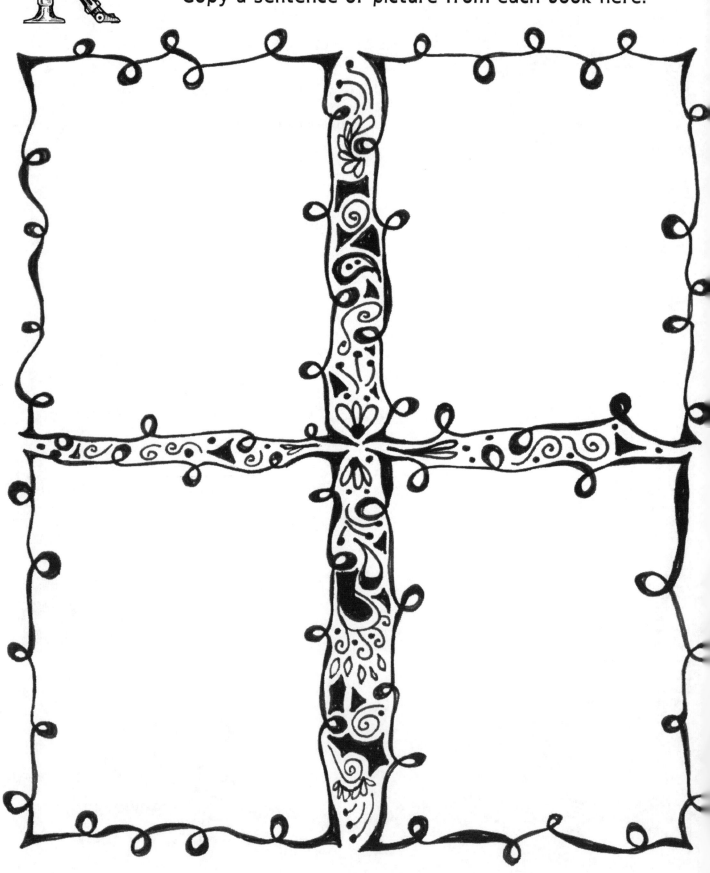

Circle Today's Date

January
February
March
April
May
June
July
August
September
October
November
December

1 2 3 4 5 6
7 8 9 10 11
12 13 14 15
16 17 18 19
20 21 22 23
24 25 26 27
28 29 30 31

MONDAY
TUESDAY
WEDNESDAY
THURSDAY
FRIDAY
SATURDAY
SUNDAY

2015
2016
2017
2018
2019
2020
2021
2022
2023
2024
2025
2026
2027
2028
2029

Write Today's Date: _ _ _ _ _ _ _ _ _ _ _ _ _ _ _ _ _

Spelling Time

Find 20 Words with 3 letters each.
Look in your books for words.
Write the words here:

_____   _____

_____   _____

_____   _____

_____   _____

_____   _____

_____   _____

_____   _____

_____   _____

_____   _____

_____   _____

Film Study

Watch a Documentary, Educational Program, Movie, or YouTube Tutorial.

TIME:

TITLE:

TOPIC: _____

I learned:_____

_____

_____

_____

NOTES:

Draw a Scene From the Film:

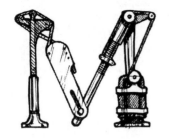

Math Practice

You can design something. You can make graphs, maps, or geometric designs. You can practice math problems.

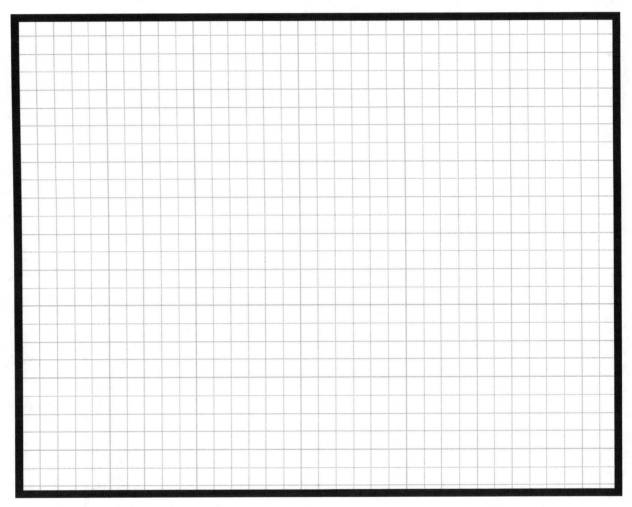

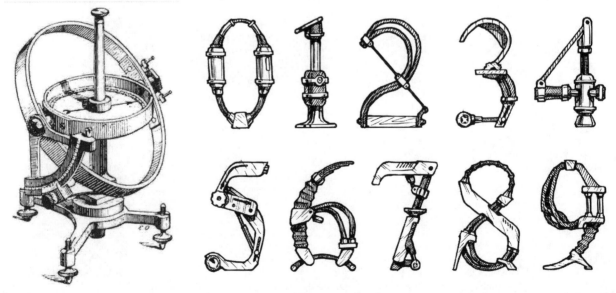

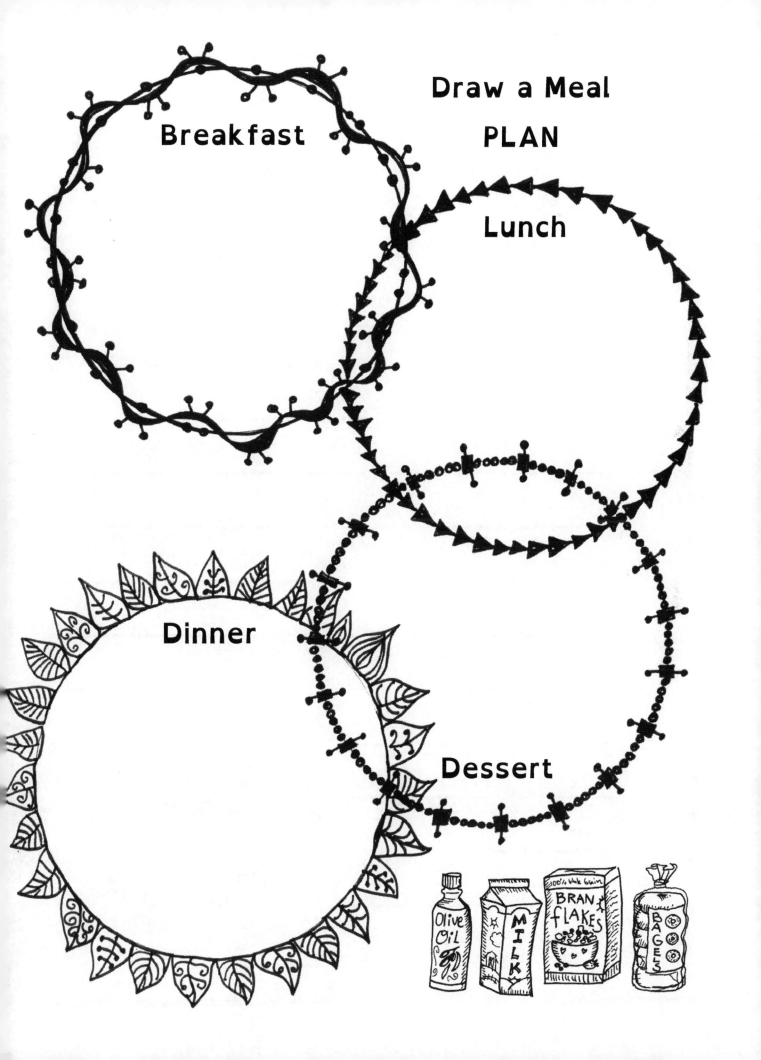

Copywork

Find an interesting paragraph in one of your books and copy it. Be diligent to make your writing look exactly like it does the book.

TITLE:_____

Page Number:_____

_____

_____

_____

_____

_____

_____

_____

_____

_____

_____

 Creative
Coloring Time

Circle Today's Date

January
February
March
April
May
June
July
August
September
October
November
December

1 2 3 4 5 6
7 8 9 10 11
12 13 14 15
16 17 18 19
20 21 22 23
24 25 26 27
28 29 30 31

MONDAY
TUESDAY
WEDNESDAY
THURSDAY
FRIDAY
SATURDAY
SUNDAY

2015
2016
2017
2018
2019
2020
2021
2022
2023
2024
2025
2026
2027
2028
2029

Write Today's Date:_ _ _ _ _ _ _ _ _ _ _ _ _ _ _ _

Write down an inspirational quote:

My Goals

To-Do List

_____

_____

_____

_____

_____

_____

Art & Letter Fun

Observation Time

Look at the object in the picture.

Do you know what it is?

Yes / No / Unsure

Write down four facts or observations

about the object.

1. _____

2. _____

3. _____

4. _____

Emotions & Moods

How are your feeling today?
Color the facial expressions
to match today's moods.

Can you of three things that might help your mood improve?

1.
2.
3.

Nature Study

Go outside and make a realistic drawing of something you find in in nature.

Reading Time - 1 Hour

Choose Four Books - Read from each book for 15 minutes.

Copy a sentence or picture from each book here:

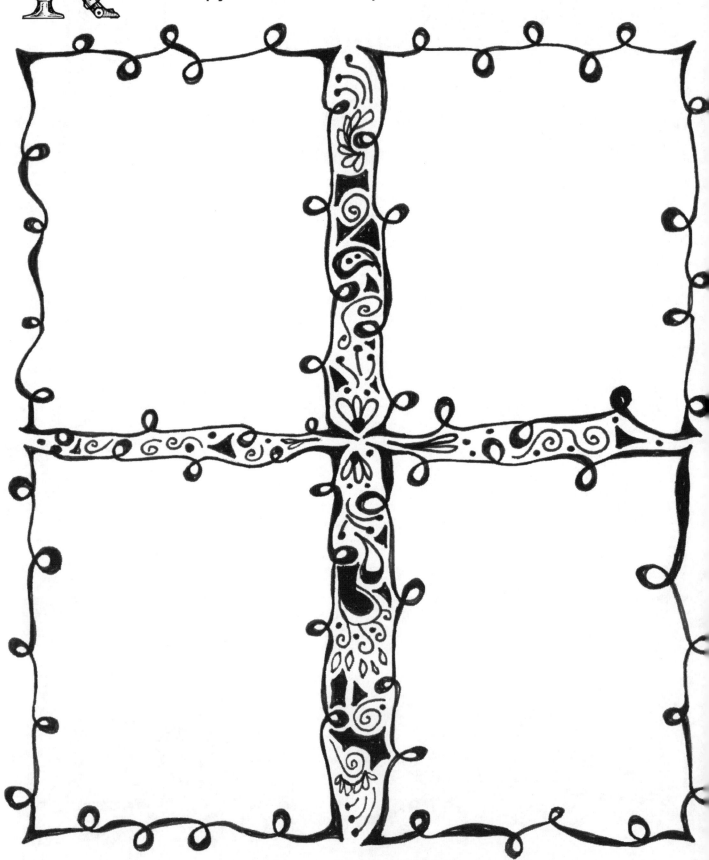

Circle Today's Date

January
February
March
April
May
June
July
August
September
October
November
December

1 2 3 4 5 6
7 8 9 10 11
12 13 14 15
16 17 18 19
20 21 22 23
24 25 26 27
28 29 30 31

MONDAY
TUESDAY
WEDNESDAY
THURSDAY
FRIDAY
SATURDAY
SUNDAY

2015
2016
2017
2018
2019
2020
2021
2022
2023
2024
2025
2026
2027
2028
2029

Write Today's Date: _____

Spelling Time

Find 20 Words with 4 letters each.
Look in your books for words.
Write the words here:

_____ _____

_____ _____

_____ _____

_____ _____

_____ _____

_____ _____

_____ _____

_____ _____

_____ _____

_____ _____

Film Study

Watch a Documentary, Educational Program, Movie, or YouTube Tutorial.

TIME:

TITLE:

TOPIC: _____

I learned: _____

_____

_____

_____

NOTES:

Draw a Scene From the Film:

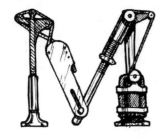

Math Practice

You can design something. You can make graphs, maps, or geometric designs. You can practice math problems.

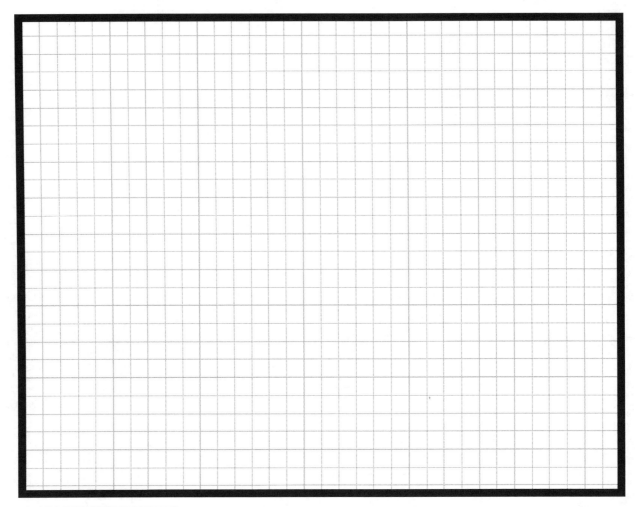

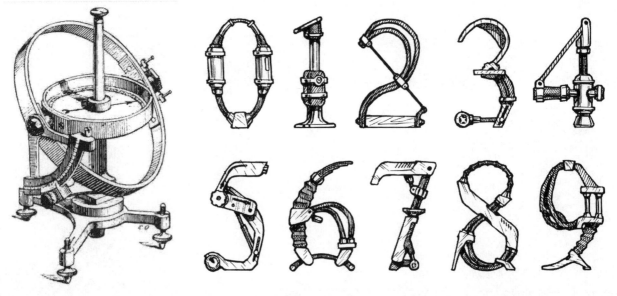

Copywork

Find an interesting paragraph in one of your books and copy it. Be diligent to make your writing look exactly like it does the book.

TITLE:_____

Page Number:_____

_____

_____

_____

_____

_____

_____

_____

_____

_____

_____

 Creative
Coloring Time

Circle Today's Date

January
February
March
April
May
June
July
August
September
October
November
December

1 2 3 4 5 6
7 8 9 10 11
12 13 14 15
16 17 18 19
20 21 22 23
24 25 26 27
28 29 30 31

MONDAY
TUESDAY
WEDNESDAY
THURSDAY
FRIDAY
SATURDAY
SUNDAY

2015
2016
2017
2018
2019
2020
2021
2022
2023
2024
2025
2026
2027
2028
2029

Write Today's Date: _ _ _ _ _ _ _ _ _ _ _ _ _ _ _ _ _

Write down an inspirational quote:

My Goals

To-Do List

_____
_____
_____
_____
_____
_____

Art & Letter Fun

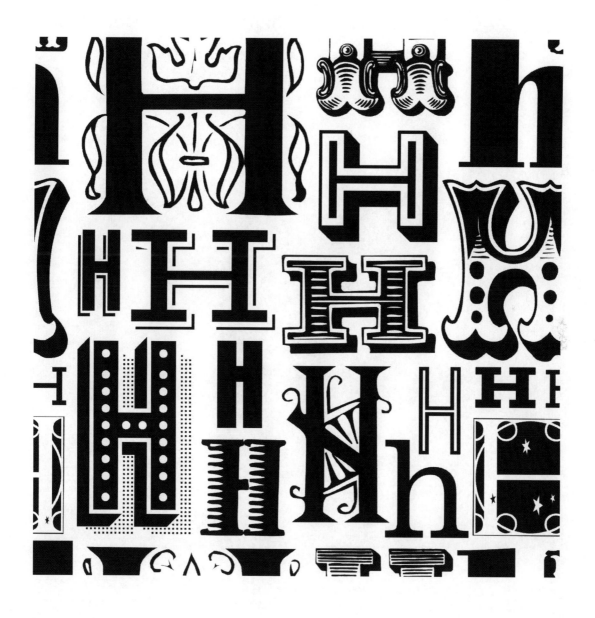

Observation Time

Look at the object in the picture.

Do you know what it is?

Yes / No / Unsure

Write down four facts or observations
about the object.

1. _____
2. _____
3. _____
4. _____

Emotions & Moods

How are your feeling today?
Color the facial expressions
to match today's moods.

Can you of three things that might help your mood improve?

1.

2.

3.

Nature Study

Go outside and make a realistic
drawing of something you find in
in nature.

Reading Time - 1 Hour

Choose Four Books - Read from each book for 15 minutes.

Copy a sentence or picture from each book here:

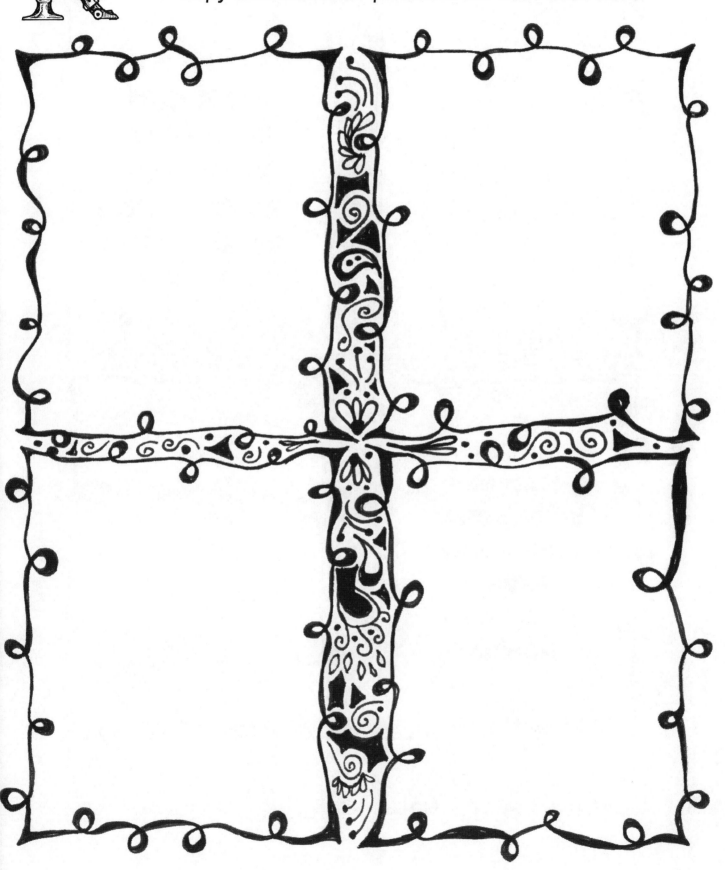

Circle Today's Date

January
February
March
April
May
June
July
August
September
October
November
December

1 2 3 4 5 6
7 8 9 10 11
12 13 14 15
16 17 18 19
20 21 22 23
24 25 26 27
28 29 30 31

MONDAY
TUESDAY
WEDNESDAY
THURSDAY
FRIDAY
SATURDAY
SUNDAY

2015
2016
2017
2018
2019
2020
2021
2022
2023
2024
2025
2026
2027
2028
2029

Write Today's Date:_____

Spelling Time

S

Find 20 Words with **5** letters each.
Look in your books for words.
Write the words here:

_____   _____

_____   _____

_____   _____

_____   _____

_____   _____

_____   _____

_____   _____

_____   _____

_____   _____

Film Study

Watch a Documentary, Educational Program, Movie, or YouTube Tutorial.

TIME:

TITLE:

TOPIC: _____

I learned:_____

_____

_____

_____

NOTES:

Draw a Scene From the Film:

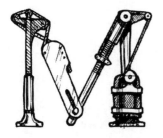

Math Practice

You can design something. You can make
graphs, maps, or geometric designs.
You can practice math problems.

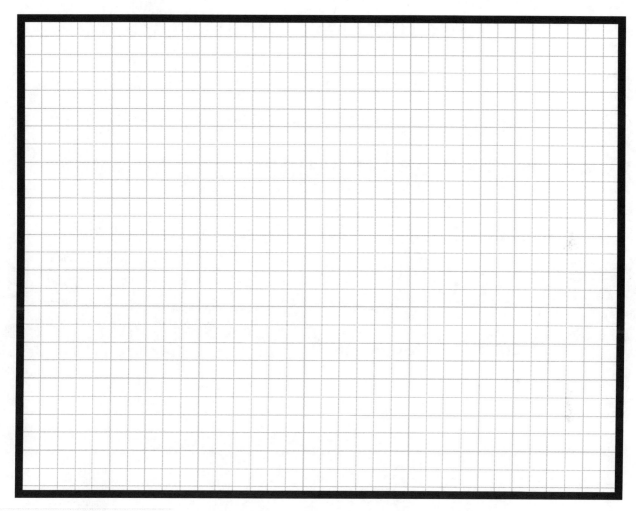

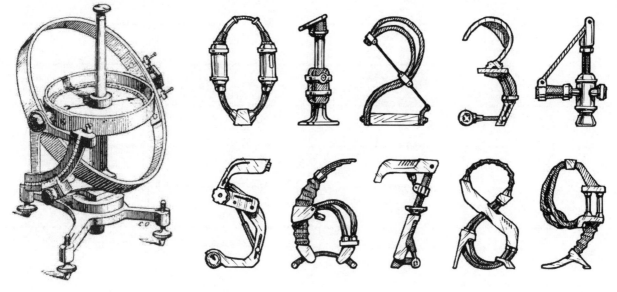

Fun Writing Practice:

ABCDEFGHIJKLMNOPQURSTUVWXYZ

abcdefghijklmnopqrstuvwxyz

ABCDEFGHIJKLMNOPQURSTUVWXYZ

ABCDEFGHIJKLMNOPQURSTUVWXYZ

abcdefghijklmnopqrstuvwxyz

Copywork

Find an interesting paragraph in one of your books and copy it. Be diligent to make your writing look exactly like it does the book.

TITLE:_____

Page Number:_____

_____

_____

_____

_____

_____

_____

_____

_____

_____

Circle Today's Date

January
February
March
April
May
June
July
August
September
October
November
December

1 2 3 4 5 6
7 8 9 10 11
12 13 14 15
16 17 18 19
20 21 22 23
24 25 26 27
28 29 30 31

MONDAY
TUESDAY
WEDNESDAY
THURSDAY
FRIDAY
SATURDAY
SUNDAY

2015
2016
2017
2018
2019
2020
2021
2022
2023
2024
2025
2026
2027
2028
2029

Write Today's Date: _ _ _ _ _ _ _ _ _ _ _ _ _ _ _ _

Write down an inspirational quote:

My Goals

To-Do List

_____

_____

_____

_____

_____

_____

Art & Letter Fun

Observation Time

Look at the object in the picture.

Do you know what it is?

Yes / No / Unsure

Write down four facts or observations

about the object.

1. _____
2. _____
3. _____
4. _____

Emotions & Moods

How are your feeling today?
Color the facial expressions
to match today's moods.

Can you of three things that might help your mood improve?

1.
2.
3.

Nature Study

Go outside and make a realistic drawing of something you find in in nature.

Reading Time - 1 Hour

Choose Four Books - Read from each book for 15 minutes.

Copy a sentence or picture from each book here:

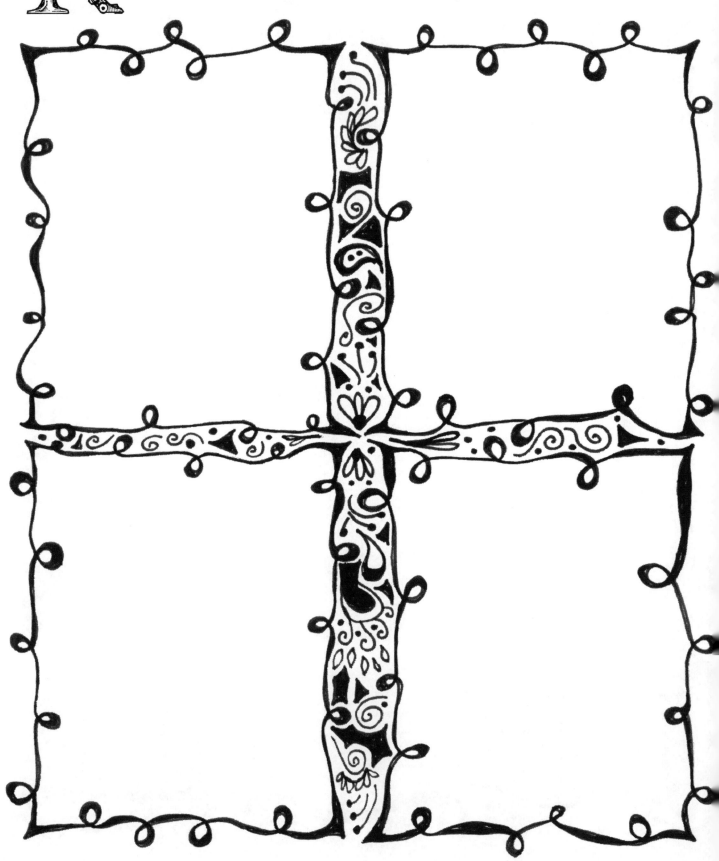

Circle Today's Date

January
February
March
April
May
June
July
August
September
October
November
December

1 2 3 4 5 6
7 8 9 10 11
12 13 14 15
16 17 18 19
20 21 22 23
24 25 26 27
28 29 30 31

MONDAY
TUESDAY
WEDNESDAY
THURSDAY
FRIDAY
SATURDAY
SUNDAY

2015
2016
2017
2018
2019
2020
2021
2022
2023
2024
2025
2026
2027
2028
2029

Write Today's Date: _ _ _ _ _ _ _ _ _ _ _ _ _ _ _

Spelling Time

Find 20 Words with **6** letters each.
Look in your books for words.
Write the words here:

_____   _____

_____   _____

_____   _____

_____   _____

_____   _____

_____   _____

_____   _____

_____   _____

_____   _____

_____   _____

Film Study

Watch a Documentary, Educational Program, Movie, or YouTube Tutorial.

TIME:

TITLE:

TOPIC: _____

I learned:_____

_____

_____

_____

NOTES:

Draw a Scene From the Film:

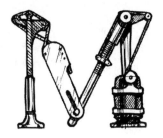

Math Practice

You can design something. You can make
graphs, maps, or geometric designs.
You can practice math problems.

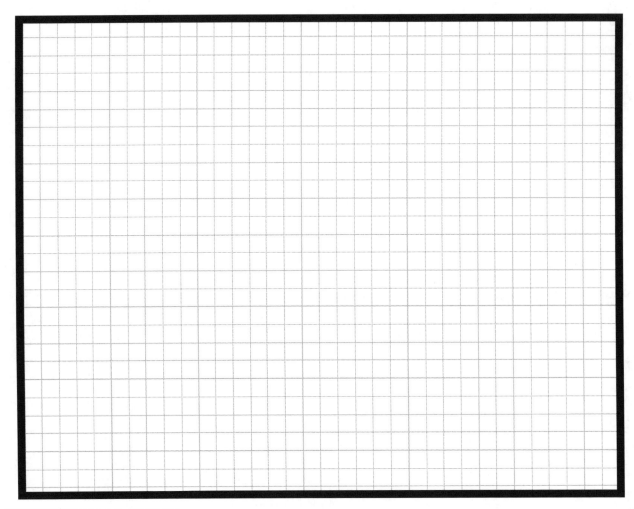

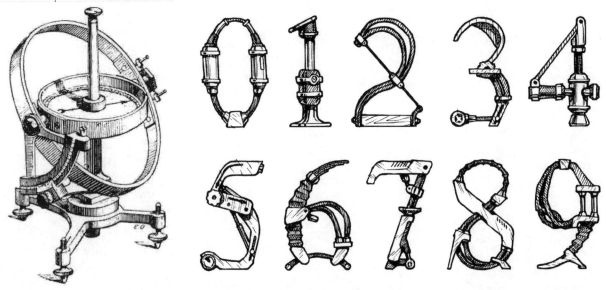

World News Today!

Talk to your parents about current events.

Look at a newspaper, news broadcast or website.

Color the countries your learn about.

Tell the news stories with words or pictures.

Copywork

Find an interesting paragraph in one of your books and copy it. Be diligent to make your writing look exactly like it does the book.

TITLE: _____

Page Number: _____

_____

_____

_____

_____

_____

_____

_____

_____

_____

Creative
Coloring Time

Circle Today's Date

January
February
March
April
May
June
July
August
September
October
November
December

1 2 3 4 5 6
7 8 9 10 11
12 13 14 15
16 17 18 19
20 21 22 23
24 25 26 27
28 29 30 31

MONDAY
TUESDAY
WEDNESDAY
THURSDAY
FRIDAY
SATURDAY
SUNDAY

2015
2016
2017
2018
2019
2020
2021
2022
2023
2024
2025
2026
2027
2028
2029

Write Today's Date: _ _ _ _ _ _ _ _ _ _ _ _ _

Write down an inspirational quote:

My Goals

To-Do List

_____
_____
_____
_____
_____
_____

Art & Letter Fun

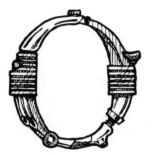

Observation Time

Look at the object in the picture.

Do you know what it is?

Yes / No / Unsure

Write down four facts or observations
about the object.

1. _____

2. _____

3. _____

4. _____

Emotions & Moods

How are your feeling today?
Color the facial expressions
to match today's moods.

Can you of three things that might help your mood improve?

1.
2.
3.

Nature Study

Go outside and make a realistic drawing of something you find in in nature.

Reading Time - 1 Hour

Choose Four Books - Read from each book for 15 minutes.

Copy a sentence or picture from each book here:

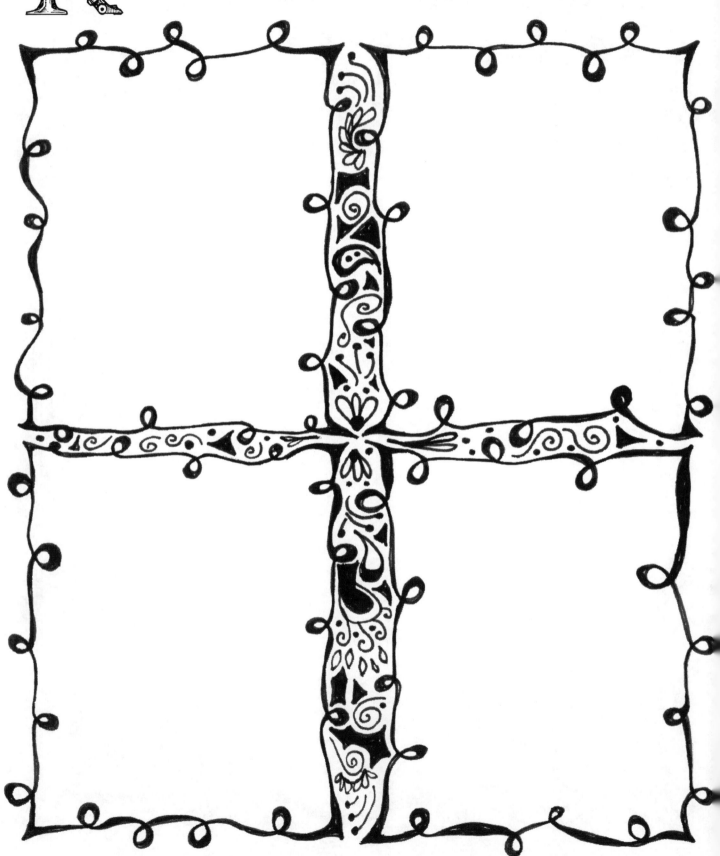

Circle Today's Date

January
February
March
April
May
June
July
August
September
October
November
December

1 2 3 4 5 6
7 8 9 10 11
12 13 14 15
16 17 18 19
20 21 22 23
24 25 26 27
28 29 30 31

MONDAY
TUESDAY
WEDNESDAY
THURSDAY
FRIDAY
SATURDAY
SUNDAY

2015
2016
2017
2018
2019
2020
2021
2022
2023
2024
2025
2026
2027
2028
2029

Write Today's Date: _____

Spelling Time

Find 20 Words with 7 letters each.
Look in your books for words.
Write the words here:

_____   _____

_____   _____

_____   _____

_____   _____

_____   _____

_____   _____

_____   _____

_____   _____

_____   _____

_____   _____

Film Study

Watch a Documentary, Educational Program, Movie, or YouTube Tutorial.

TIME:

TITLE:

TOPIC: _____

I learned:_____

_____

_____

_____

NOTES:

Draw a Scene From the Film:

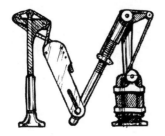

Math Practice

You can design something. You can make graphs, maps, or geometric designs. You can practice math problems.

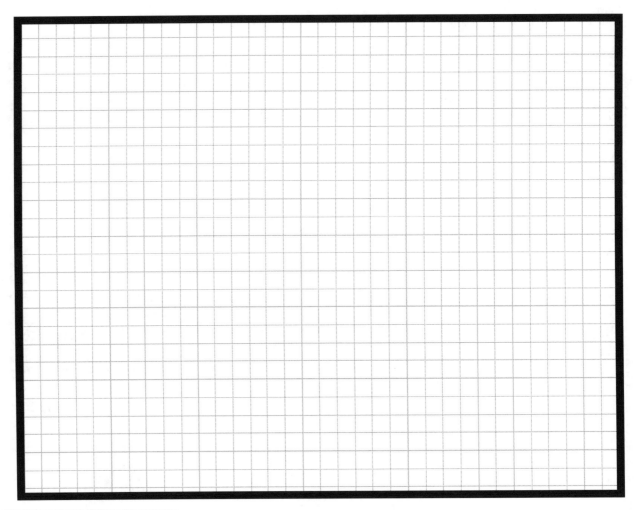

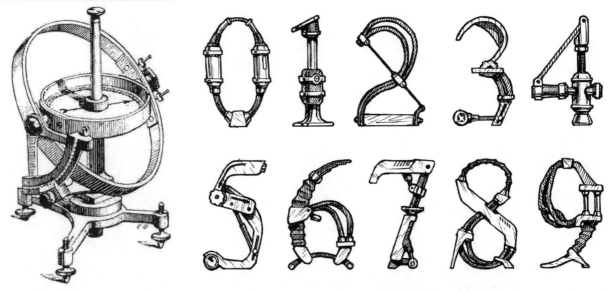

Copywork

Find an interesting paragraph in one of your books and copy it. Be diligent to make your writing look exactly like it does the book.

TITLE:_____

Page Number:_____

_____

_____

_____

_____

_____

_____

_____

_____

_____

Creative
Coloring Time

Circle Today's Date

January
February
March
April
May
June
July
August
September
October
November
December

1 2 3 4 5 6
7 8 9 10 11
12 13 14 15
16 17 18 19
20 21 22 23
24 25 26 27
28 29 30 31

MONDAY
TUESDAY
WEDNESDAY
THURSDAY
FRIDAY
SATURDAY
SUNDAY

2015
2016
2017
2018
2019
2020
2021
2022
2023
2024
2025
2026
2027
2028
2029

Write Today's Date: _ _ _ _ _ _ _ _ _ _ _ _ _ _ _ _

Write down an inspirational quote:

My Goals

To-Do List

_____
_____
_____
_____
_____
_____

Art & Letter Fun

Observation Time

Look at the object in the picture.

Do you know what it is?

Yes / No / Unsure

Write down four facts or observations

about the object.

1. _____
2. _____
3. _____
4. _____

Emotions & Moods

How are your feeling today?
Color the facial expressions
to match today's moods.

Can you of three things that might help your mood improve?

1.
2.
3.

Nature Study

Go outside and make a realistic
drawing of something you find in
in nature.

Reading Time - 1 Hour

Choose Four Books - Read from each book for 15 minutes.

Copy a sentence or picture from each book here:

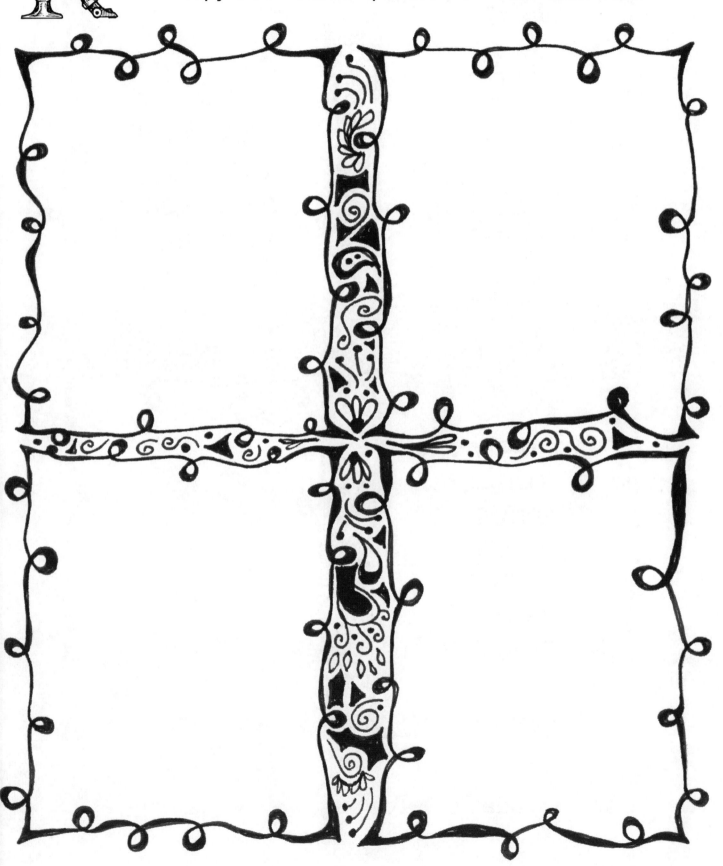

Circle Today's Date

January
February
March
April
May
June
July
August
September
October
November
December

1 2 3 4 5 6
7 8 9 10 11
12 13 14 15
16 17 18 19
20 21 22 23
24 25 26 27
28 29 30 31

MONDAY
TUESDAY
WEDNESDAY
THURSDAY
FRIDAY
SATURDAY
SUNDAY

2015
2016
2017
2018
2019
2020
2021
2022
2023
2024
2025
2026
2027
2028
2029

Write Today's Date: _ _ _ _ _ _ _ _ _ _ _ _ _ _ _ _ _

Spelling Time

Find 20 Words with **8** letters each.

Look in your books for words.

Write the words here:

_____   _____

_____   _____

_____   _____

_____   _____

_____   _____

_____   _____

_____   _____

_____   _____

_____   _____

Film Study

Watch a Documentary, Educational Program, Movie, or YouTube Tutorial.

TIME:

TITLE:

TOPIC: _____

I learned:_____

_____

_____

_____

NOTES:

Draw a Scene From the Film:

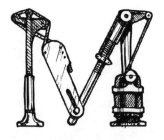

Math Practice

You can design something. You can make
graphs, maps, or geometric designs.
You can practice math problems.

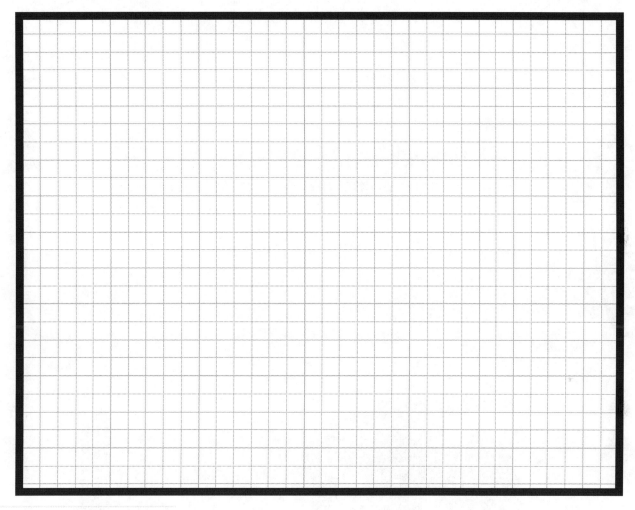

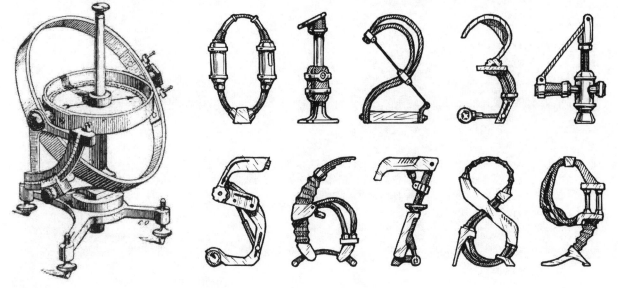

Listening Time

Listen to an audio book or classical music or ask someone to read a story to you while you color and draw on the next page.

What are you listening to?

_____

Creative
Coloring Time

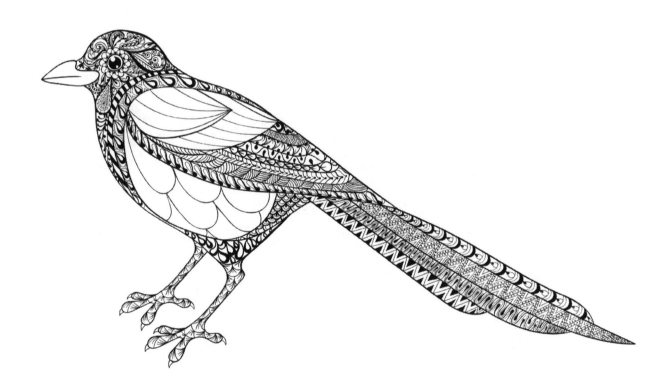

Circle Today's Date

January
February
March
April
May
June
July
August
September
October
November
December

1 2 3 4 5 6
7 8 9 10 11
12 13 14 15
16 17 18 19
20 21 22 23
24 25 26 27
28 29 30 31

MONDAY
TUESDAY
WEDNESDAY
THURSDAY
FRIDAY
SATURDAY
SUNDAY

2015
2016
2017
2018
2019
2020
2021
2022
2023
2024
2025
2026
2027
2028
2029

Write Today's Date:_____

Write down an inspirational quote:

My Goals

To-Do List

Art & Letter Fun

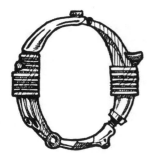

Observation Time

Look at the object in the picture.

Do you know what it is?

Yes / No / Unsure

Write down four facts or observations

about the object.

1. _____
2. _____
3. _____
4. _____

Emotions & Moods

How are your feeling today?
Color the facial expressions
to match today's moods.

Can you of three things that might help your mood improve?

1.

2.

3.

Nature Study

Go outside and make a realistic drawing of something you find in in nature.

Reading Time - 1 Hour

Choose Four Books - Read from each book for 15 minutes.

Copy a sentence or picture from each book here:

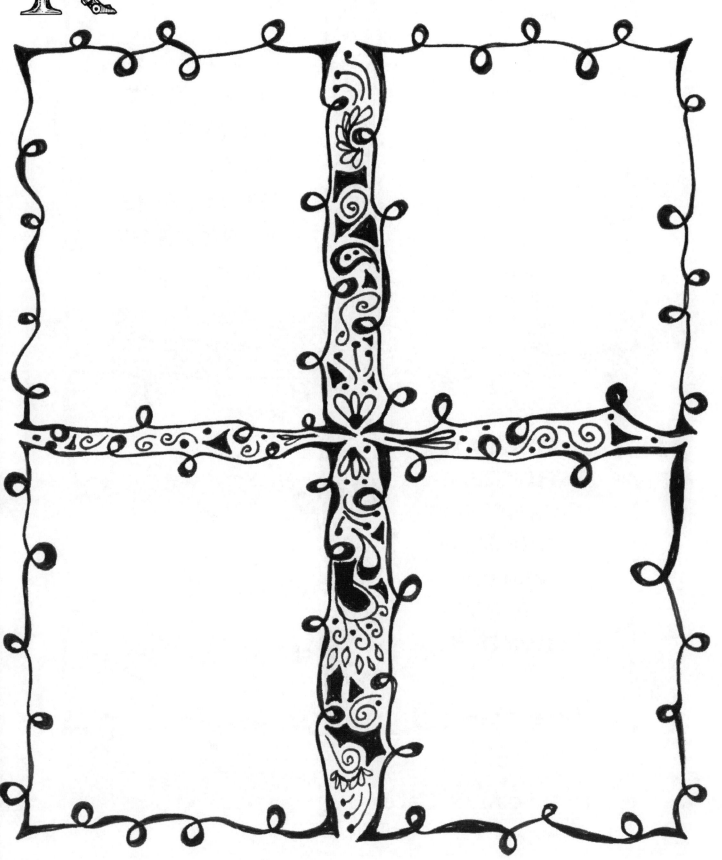

Circle Today's Date

January
February
March
April
May
June
July
August
September
October
November
December

1 2 3 4 5 6
7 8 9 10 11
12 13 14 15
16 17 18 19
20 21 22 23
24 25 26 27
28 29 30 31

MONDAY
TUESDAY
WEDNESDAY
THURSDAY
FRIDAY
SATURDAY
SUNDAY

2015
2016
2017
2018
2019
2020
2021
2022
2023
2024
2025
2026
2027
2028
2029

Write Today's Date: _ _ _ _ _ _ _ _ _ _ _ _ _ _ _ _

Spelling Time

Find 20 Words with **9** letters each.

Look in your books for words.

Write the words here:

_____   _____

_____   _____

_____   _____

_____   _____

_____   _____

_____   _____

_____   _____

_____   _____

_____   _____

_____   _____

Film Study

Watch a Documentary, Educational Program, Movie, or YouTube Tutorial.

TIME:

TITLE:

TOPIC: _____

I learned:_____

_____

_____

_____

NOTES:

Draw a Scene From the Film:

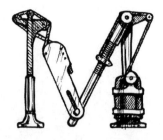

Math Practice

You can design something. You can make
graphs, maps, or geometric designs.
You can practice math problems.

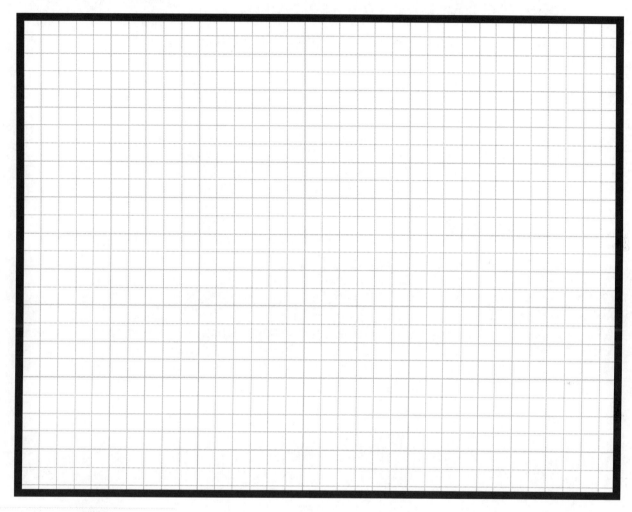

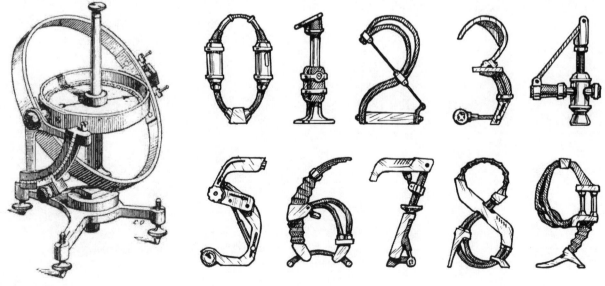

World News Today!

Talk to your parents about current events.
Look at a newspaper, news broadcast or website.
Color the countries your learn about.
Tell the news stories with words or pictures.

Copywork

Find an interesting paragraph in one of your books and copy it. Be diligent to make your writing look exactly like it does the book.

TITLE:_____

Page Number:_____

_____

_____

_____

_____

_____

_____

_____

_____

_____

 Creative

Coloring Time

Circle Today's Date

January
February
March
April
May
June
July
August
September
October
November
December

1 2 3 4 5 6
7 8 9 10 11
12 13 14 15
16 17 18 19
20 21 22 23
24 25 26 27
28 29 30 31

MONDAY
TUESDAY
WEDNESDAY
THURSDAY
FRIDAY
SATURDAY
SUNDAY

2015
2016
2017
2018
2019
2020
2021
2022
2023
2024
2025
2026
2027
2028
2029

Write Today's Date:_____

Write down an inspirational quote:

My Goals

To-Do List

_____
_____
_____
_____
_____
_____

Art & Letter Fun

Observation Time

Look at the object in the picture.

Do you know what it is?

Yes / No / Unsure

Write down four facts or observations
about the object.

1. _____
2. _____
3. _____
4. _____

Emotions & Moods

How are your feeling today?
Color the facial expressions
to match today's moods.

Can you of three things that might help your mood improve?

1.
2.
3.

Nature Study

Go outside and make a realistic drawing of something you find in in nature.

Reading Time - 1 Hour

Choose Four Books - Read from each book for 15 minutes.

Copy a sentence or picture from each book here:

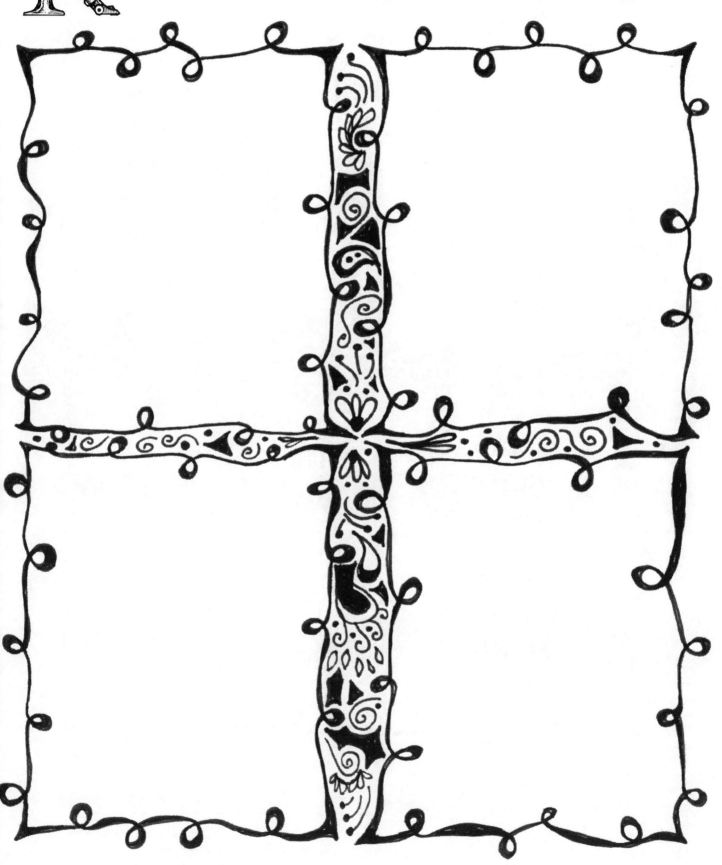

Circle Today's Date

January
February
March
April
May
June
July
August
September
October
November
December

1 2 3 4 5 6
7 8 9 10 11
12 13 14 15
16 17 18 19
20 21 22 23
24 25 26 27
28 29 30 31

MONDAY
TUESDAY
WEDNESDAY
THURSDAY
FRIDAY
SATURDAY
SUNDAY

2015
2016
2017
2018
2019
2020
2021
2022
2023
2024
2025
2026
2027
2028
2029

Write Today's Date:_____

Spelling Time

Find 20 Words with **8** letters each.

Look in your books for words.

Write the words here:

_____   _____

_____   _____

_____   _____

_____   _____

_____   _____

_____   _____

_____   _____

_____   _____

_____   _____

Film Study

Watch a Documentary, Educational Program, Movie, or YouTube Tutorial.

TIME:

TITLE:

TOPIC: _____

I learned:_____

_____

_____

_____

NOTES:

Draw a Scene From the Film:

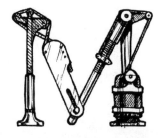

Math Practice

You can design something. You can make
graphs, maps, or geometric designs.
You can practice math problems.

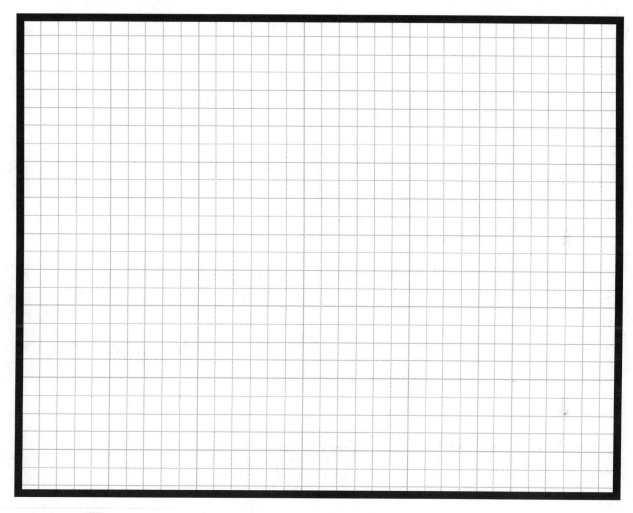

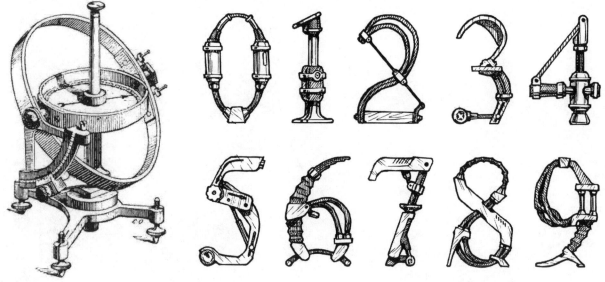

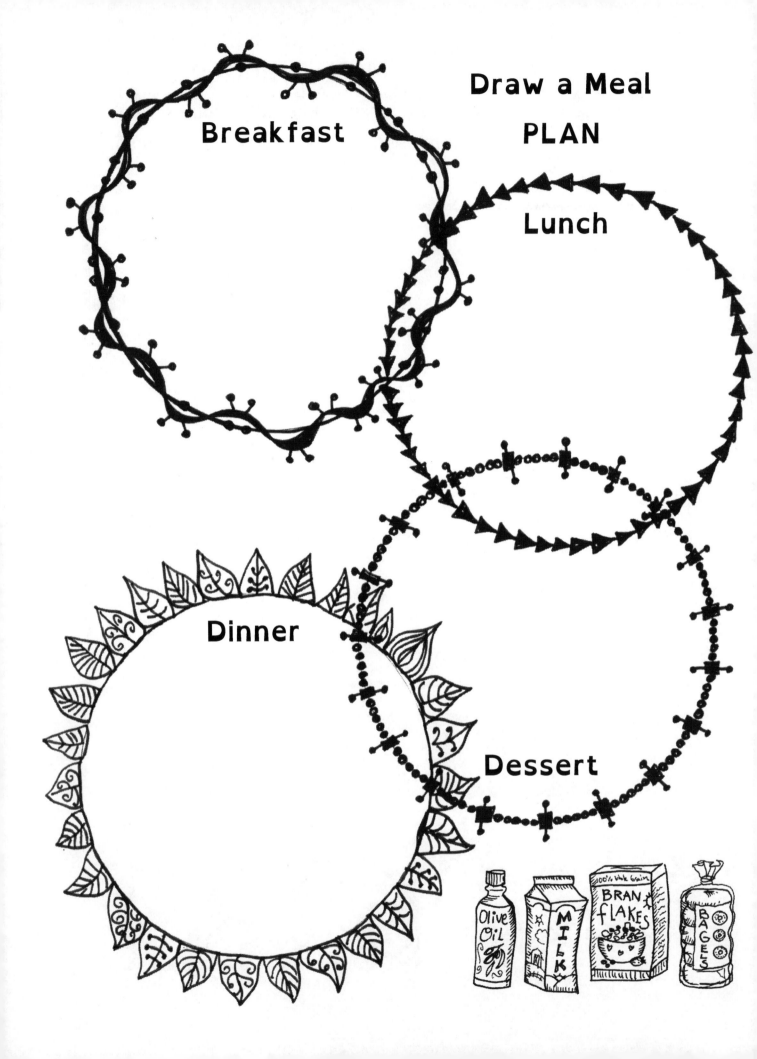

Copywork

Find an interesting paragraph in one of your books and copy it. Be diligent to make your writing look exactly like it does the book.

TITLE:_____

Page Number:_____

_____

_____

_____

_____

_____

_____

_____

_____

_____

_____

Circle Today's Date

January
February
March
April
May
June
July
August
September
October
November
December

1 2 3 4 5 6
7 8 9 10 11
12 13 14 15
16 17 18 19
20 21 22 23
24 25 26 27
28 29 30 31

MONDAY
TUESDAY
WEDNESDAY
THURSDAY
FRIDAY
SATURDAY
SUNDAY

2015
2016
2017
2018
2019
2020
2021
2022
2023
2024
2025
2026
2027
2028
2029

Write Today's Date: _____

Write down an inspirational quote:

My Goals

To-Do List

_____
_____
_____
_____
_____
_____

Art & Letter Fun

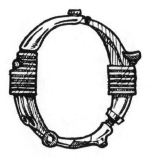

Observation Time

Look at the object in the picture.

Do you know what it is?

Yes / No / Unsure

Write down four facts or observations

about the object.

1. _____
2. _____
3. _____
4. _____

Emotions & Moods

How are your feeling today?

Color the facial expressions

to match today's moods.

Can you of three things that might help your mood improve?

1.

2.

3.

Nature Study

Go outside and make a realistic drawing of something you find in in nature.

Reading Time - 1 Hour

Choose Four Books - Read from each book for 15 minutes.

Copy a sentence or picture from each book here:

Circle Today's Date

January
February
March
April
May
June
July
August
September
October
November
December

1 2 3 4 5 6
7 8 9 10 11
12 13 14 15
16 17 18 19
20 21 22 23
24 25 26 27
28 29 30 31

MONDAY
TUESDAY
WEDNESDAY
THURSDAY
FRIDAY
SATURDAY
SUNDAY

2015
2016
2017
2018
2019
2020
2021
2022
2023
2024
2025
2026
2027
2028
2029

Write Today's Date:_____

Spelling Time

Find 20 Words with **8** letters each.
Look in your books for words.
Write the words here:

Film Study

Watch a Documentary, Educational Program, Movie, or YouTube Tutorial.

TIME:

TITLE:

TOPIC: _____

I learned:_____

_____

_____

_____

NOTES:

Draw a Scene From the Film:

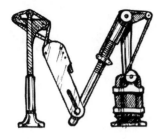

Math Practice

You can design something. You can make
graphs, maps, or geometric designs.
You can practice math problems.

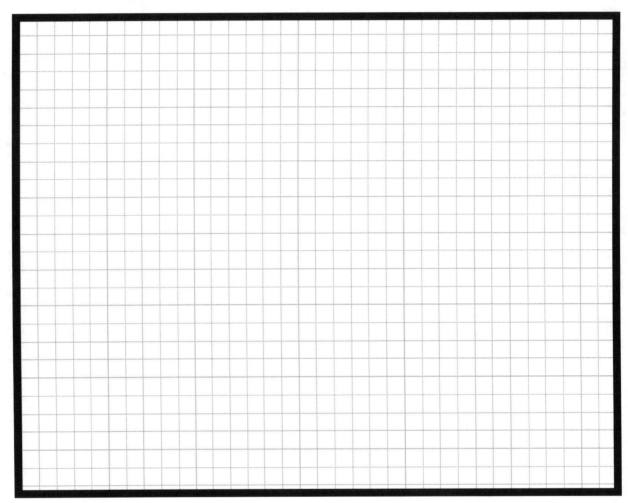

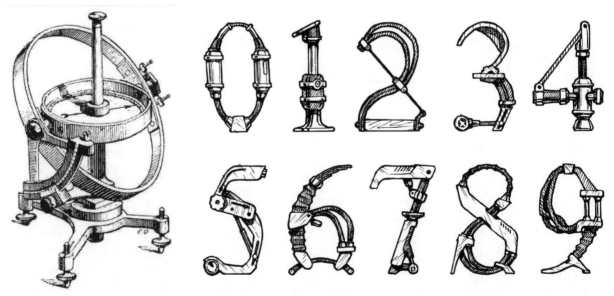

Copywork

Find an interesting paragraph in one of your books and copy it. Be diligent to make your writing look exactly like it does the book.

TITLE:_____

Page Number:_____

_____

_____

_____

_____

_____

_____

_____

_____

_____

Creative
Coloring Time

Circle Today's Date

January
February
March
April
May
June
July
August
September
October
November
December

1 2 3 4 5 6
7 8 9 10 11
12 13 14 15
16 17 18 19
20 21 22 23
24 25 26 27
28 29 30 31

MONDAY
TUESDAY
WEDNESDAY
THURSDAY
FRIDAY
SATURDAY
SUNDAY

2015
2016
2017
2018
2019
2020
2021
2022
2023
2024
2025
2026
2027
2028
2029

Write Today's Date:_____

Write down an inspirational quote:

My Goals

To-Do List

_____
_____
_____
_____
_____
_____

Art & Letter Fun

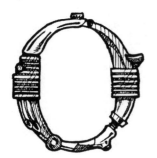

Observation Time

Look at the object in the picture.

Do you know what it is?

Yes / No / Unsure

Write down four facts or observations

about the object.

1. _____

2. _____

3. _____

4. _____

Nature Study

Go outside and make a realistic drawing of something you find in in nature.

Reading Time - 1 Hour

Choose Four Books - Read from each book for 15 minutes.

Copy a sentence or picture from each book here:

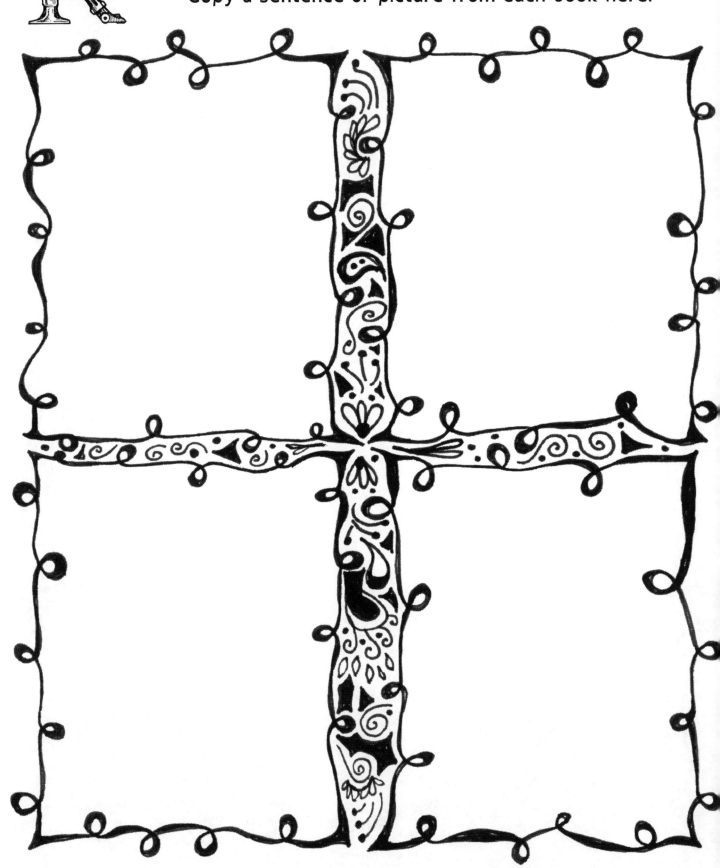

Circle Today's Date

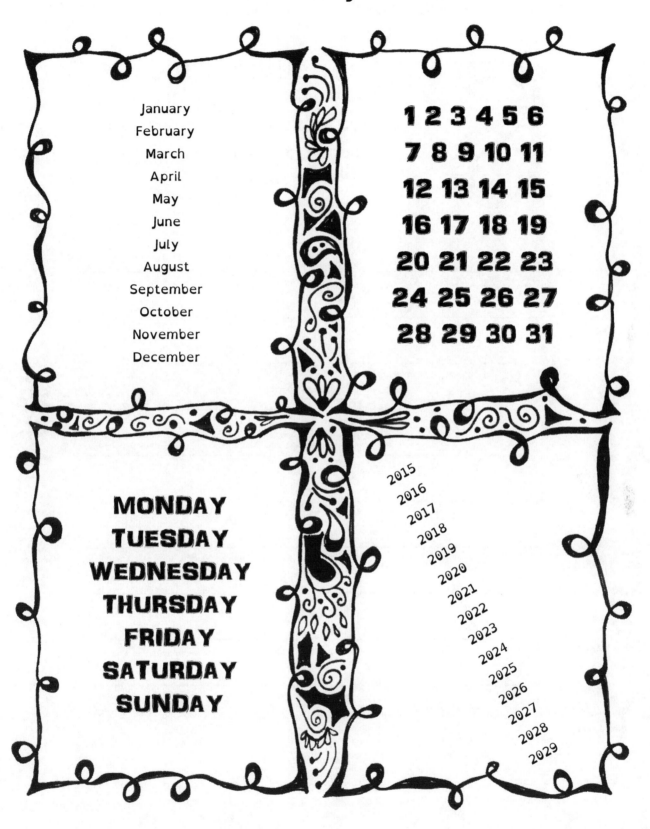

January
February
March
April
May
June
July
August
September
October
November
December

1 2 3 4 5 6
7 8 9 10 11
12 13 14 15
16 17 18 19
20 21 22 23
24 25 26 27
28 29 30 31

MONDAY
TUESDAY
WEDNESDAY
THURSDAY
FRIDAY
SATURDAY
SUNDAY

2015
2016
2017
2018
2019
2020
2021
2022
2023
2024
2025
2026
2027
2028
2029

Write Today's Date:_____

Spelling Time

Find 20 Words with **7** letters each.
Look in your books for words.
Write the words here:

_____   _____

_____   _____

_____   _____

_____   _____

_____   _____

_____   _____

_____   _____

_____   _____

_____   _____

Film Study

Watch a Documentary, Educational
Program, Movie, or YouTube Tutorial.

TIME:

TITLE:

TOPIC: _____

I learned:_____

_____

_____

_____

NOTES:

Draw a Scene From the Film:

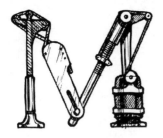

Math Practice

You can design something. You can make
graphs, maps, or geometric designs.
You can practice math problems.

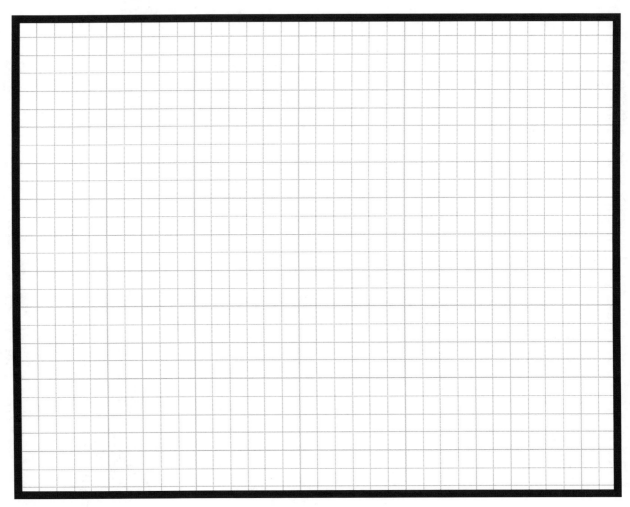

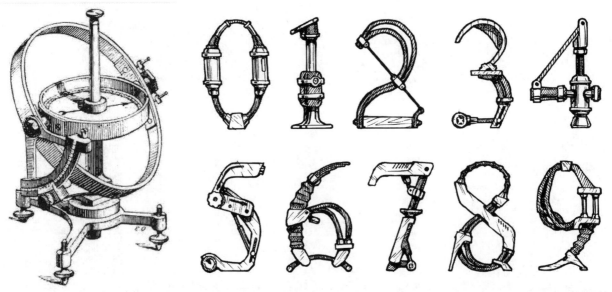

Fun Writing Practice:

ABCDEFGHIJKLMNOPQURSTUVWXYZ

abcdefghijklmnopqrstuvwxyz

ABCDEFGHIJKLMNOPQURSTUVWXYZ

ABCDEFGHIJKLMNOPQURSTUVWXYZ

abcdefghijklmnopqrstuvwxyz

Copywork

Find an interesting paragraph in one of your books and copy it. Be diligent to make your writing look exactly like it does the book.

TITLE:_____

Page Number:_____

_____

_____

_____

_____

_____

_____

_____

_____

_____

_____

Circle Today's Date

January
February
March
April
May
June
July
August
September
October
November
December

1 2 3 4 5 6
7 8 9 10 11
12 13 14 15
16 17 18 19
20 21 22 23
24 25 26 27
28 29 30 31

MONDAY
TUESDAY
WEDNESDAY
THURSDAY
FRIDAY
SATURDAY
SUNDAY

2015
2016
2017
2018
2019
2020
2021
2022
2023
2024
2025
2026
2027
2028
2029

Write Today's Date: _____

Write down an inspirational quote:

My Goals

To-Do List

_____
_____
_____
_____
_____
_____

Art & Letter Fun

Observation Time

Look at the object in the picture.

Do you know what it is?

Yes / No / Unsure

Write down four facts or observations

about the object.

1. _____
2. _____
3. _____
4. _____

Emotions & Moods

How are your feeling today?
Color the facial expressions
to match today's moods.

Can you of three things that might help your mood improve?

1.
2.
3.

Circle Today's Date

January
February
March
April
May
June
July
August
September
October
November
December

1 2 3 4 5 6
7 8 9 10 11
12 13 14 15
16 17 18 19
20 21 22 23
24 25 26 27
28 29 30 31

MONDAY
TUESDAY
WEDNESDAY
THURSDAY
FRIDAY
SATURDAY
SUNDAY

2015
2016
2017
2018
2019
2020
2021
2022
2023
2024
2025
2026
2027
2028
2029

Write Today's Date:_____

Nature Study

Go outside and make a realistic drawing of something you find in in nature.

Reading Time - 1 Hour

Choose Four Books - Read from each book for 15 minutes.

Copy a sentence or picture from each book here:

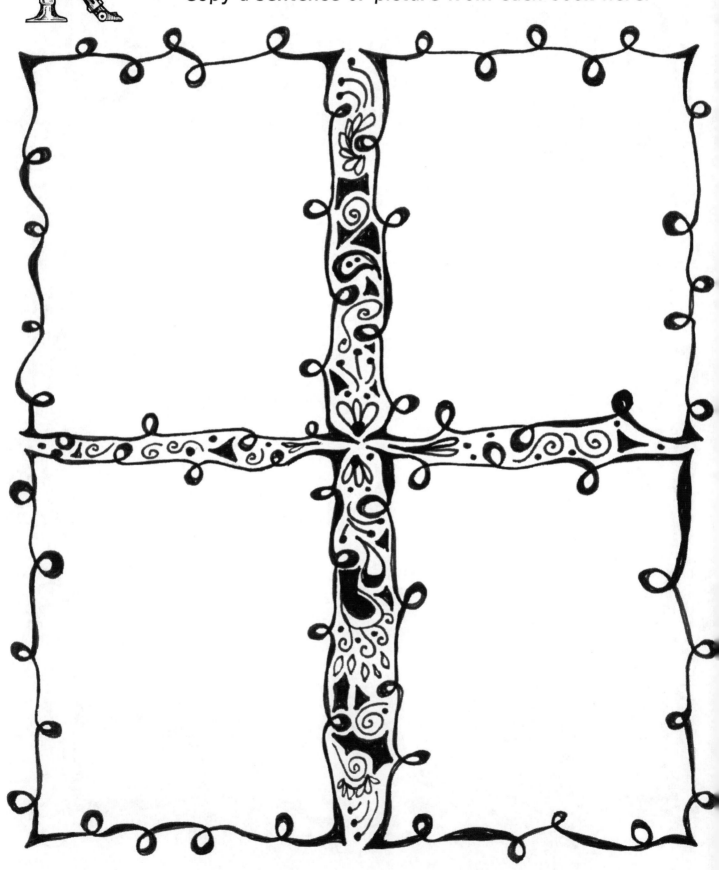

Spelling Time

Find 20 Words with 6 letters each.
Look in your books for words.
Write the words here:

_____   _____

_____   _____

_____   _____

_____   _____

_____   _____

_____   _____

_____   _____

_____   _____

_____   _____

_____   _____

Film Study

Watch a Documentary, Educational Program, Movie, or YouTube Tutorial.

TIME:

TITLE:

TOPIC: _____

I learned:_____

_____

_____

_____

NOTES:

Draw a Scene From the Film:

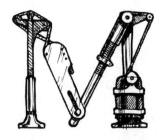

Math Practice

You can design something. You can make
graphs, maps, or geometric designs.
You can practice math problems.

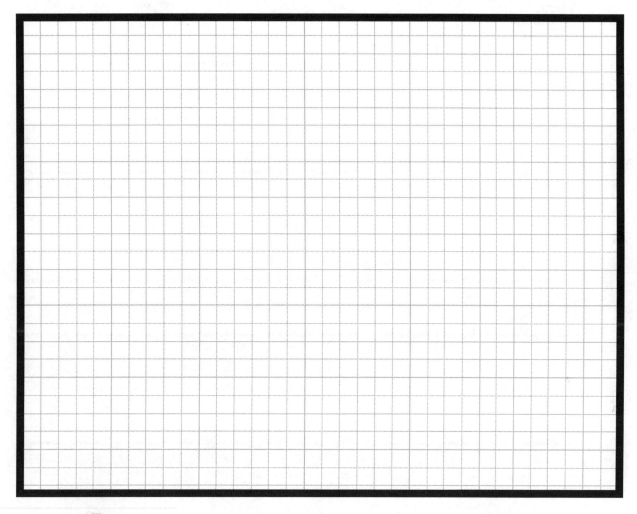

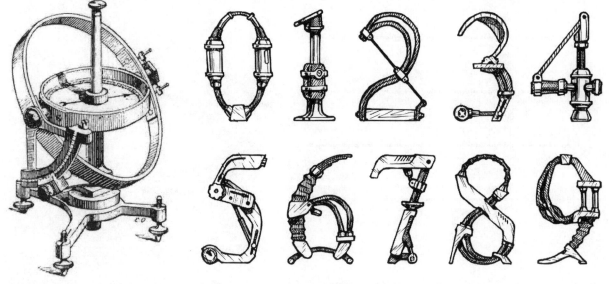

Copywork

Find an interesting paragraph in one of your books and copy it. Be diligent to make your writing look exactly like it does the book.

TITLE:_____

Page Number:_____

_____

_____

_____

_____

_____

_____

_____

_____

_____

Creative
Coloring Time

Circle Today's Date

January
February
March
April
May
June
July
August
September
October
November
December

1 2 3 4 5 6
7 8 9 10 11
12 13 14 15
16 17 18 19
20 21 22 23
24 25 26 27
28 29 30 31

MONDAY
TUESDAY
WEDNESDAY
THURSDAY
FRIDAY
SATURDAY
SUNDAY

2015
2016
2017
2018
2019
2020
2021
2022
2023
2024
2025
2026
2027
2028
2029

Write Today's Date: _ _ _ _ _ _ _ _ _ _ _ _ _ _ _ _

Write down an inspirational quote:

My Goals

To-Do List

_____
_____
_____
_____
_____
_____

Art & Letter Fun

Observation Time

Look at the object in the picture.

Do you know what it is?

Yes / No / Unsure

Write down four facts or observations
about the object.

1. _____
2. _____
3. _____
4. _____

Emotions & Moods

How are your feeling today?

Color the facial expressions

to match today's moods.

Can you of three things that might help your mood improve?

1.
2.
3.

Nature Study

Go outside and make a realistic drawing of something you find in in nature.

Circle Today's Date

January
February
March
April
May
June
July
August
September
October
November
December

1 2 3 4 5 6
7 8 9 10 11
12 13 14 15
16 17 18 19
20 21 22 23
24 25 26 27
28 29 30 31

MONDAY
TUESDAY
WEDNESDAY
THURSDAY
FRIDAY
SATURDAY
SUNDAY

2015
2016
2017
2018
2019
2020
2021
2022
2023
2024
2025
2026
2027
2028
2029

Write Today's Date: _____

Reading Time - 1 Hour

Choose Four Books - Read from each book for 15 minutes.

Copy a sentence or picture from each book here:

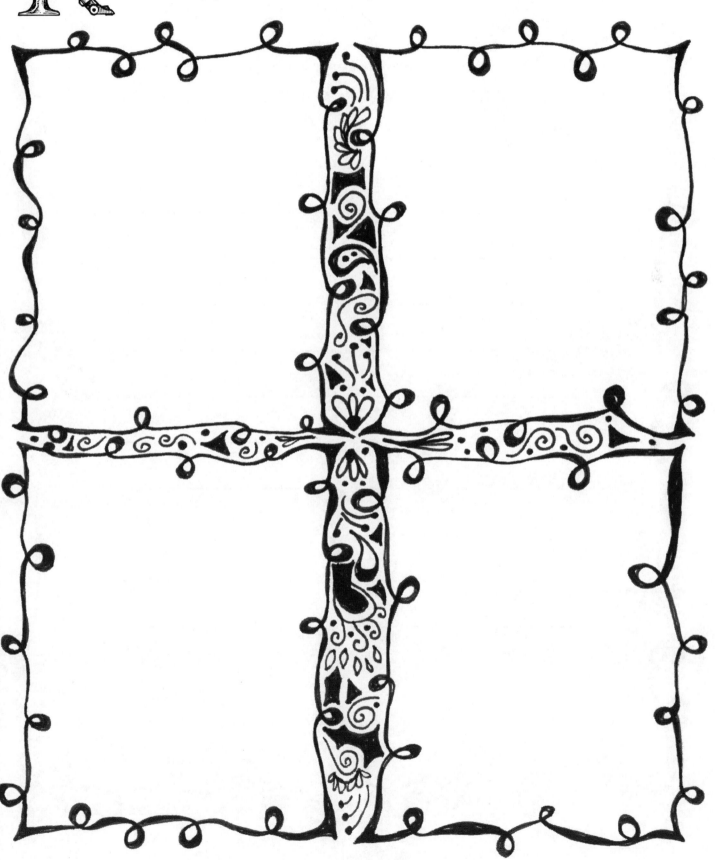

Spelling Time

Find 20 Words with 5 letters each.
Look in your books for words.
Write the words here:

Film Study

Watch a Documentary, Educational Program, Movie, or YouTube Tutorial.

TIME:

TITLE:

TOPIC: _____

I learned:_____

_____

_____

_____

NOTES:

Draw a Scene From the Film:

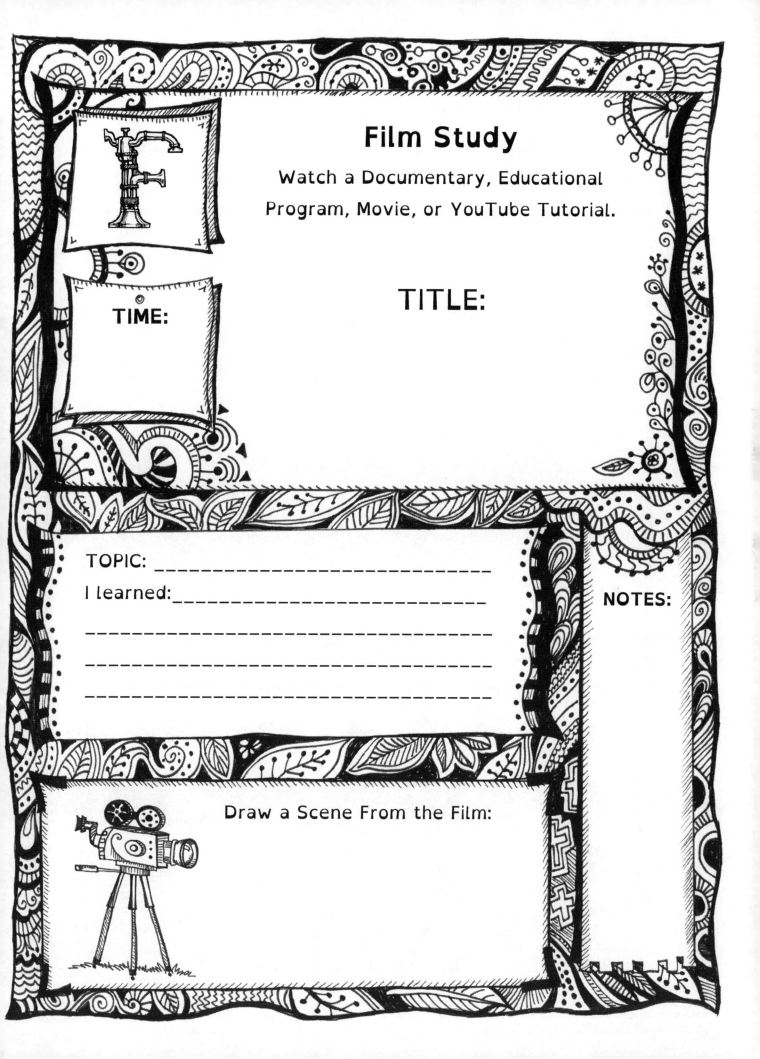

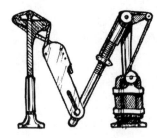

Math Practice

You can design something. You can make graphs, maps, or geometric designs. You can practice math problems.

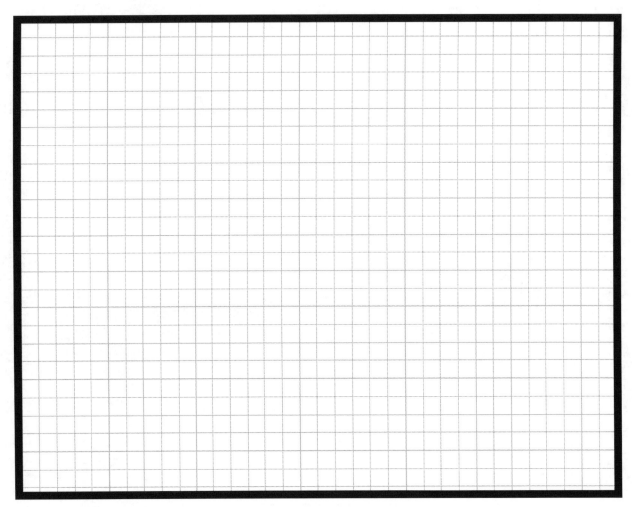

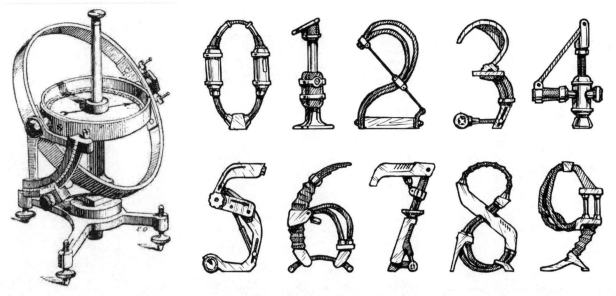

World News Today!

Talk to your parents about current events.
Look at a newspaper, news broadcast or website.
Color the countries your learn about.
Tell the news stories with words or pictures.

Copywork

Find an interesting paragraph in one of your books and copy it. Be diligent to make your writing look exactly like it does the book.

TITLE:_____

Page Number:_____

_____

_____

_____

_____

_____

_____

_____

_____

_____

 Creative
Coloring Time

Circle Today's Date

January
February
March
April
May
June
July
August
September
October
November
December

1 2 3 4 5 6
7 8 9 10 11
12 13 14 15
16 17 18 19
20 21 22 23
24 25 26 27
28 29 30 31

MONDAY
TUESDAY
WEDNESDAY
THURSDAY
FRIDAY
SATURDAY
SUNDAY

2015
2016
2017
2018
2019
2020
2021
2022
2023
2024
2025
2026
2027
2028
2029

Write Today's Date: _ _ _ _ _ _ _ _ _ _ _ _ _ _ _ _ _ _

Write down an inspirational quote:

My Goals

To-Do List

_____

_____

_____

_____

_____

_____

Art & Letter Fun

Observation Time

Look at the object in the picture.

Do you know what it is?

Yes / No / Unsure

Write down four facts or observations

about the object.

1. _____

2. _____

3. _____

4. _____

Emotions & Moods

How are your feeling today?
Color the facial expressions
to match today's moods.

Can you of three things that might help your mood improve?

1.
2.
3.

Nature Study

Go outside and make a realistic drawing of something you find in in nature.

Circle Today's Date

January
February
March
April
May
June
July
August
September
October
November
December

1 2 3 4 5 6
7 8 9 10 11
12 13 14 15
16 17 18 19
20 21 22 23
24 25 26 27
28 29 30 31

MONDAY
TUESDAY
WEDNESDAY
THURSDAY
FRIDAY
SATURDAY
SUNDAY

2015
2016
2017
2018
2019
2020
2021
2022
2023
2024
2025
2026
2027
2028
2029

Write Today's Date:_____

Reading Time - 1 Hour

Choose Four Books - Read from each book for 15 minutes.

Copy a sentence or picture from each book here:

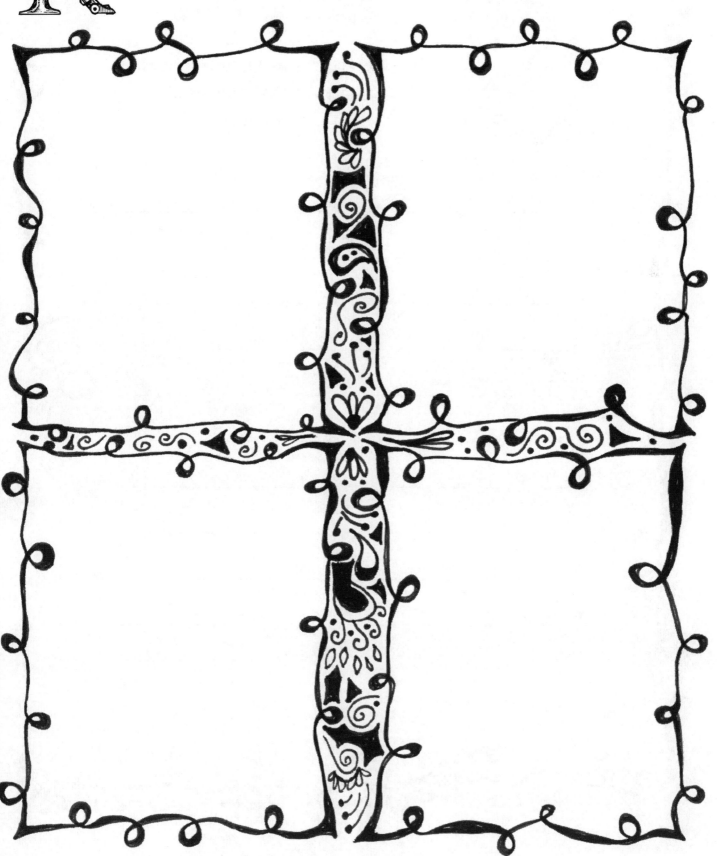

Spelling Time

S

Find 20 Words with **6** letters each.

Look in your books for words.

Write the words here:

_____   _____

_____   _____

_____   _____

_____   _____

_____   _____

_____   _____

_____   _____

_____   _____

_____   _____

_____   _____

Film Study

Watch a Documentary, Educational Program, Movie, or YouTube Tutorial.

TIME:

TITLE:

TOPIC: _____

I learned: _____

_____

_____

_____

NOTES:

Draw a Scene From the Film:

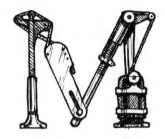

Math Practice

You can design something. You can make graphs, maps, or geometric designs. You can practice math problems.

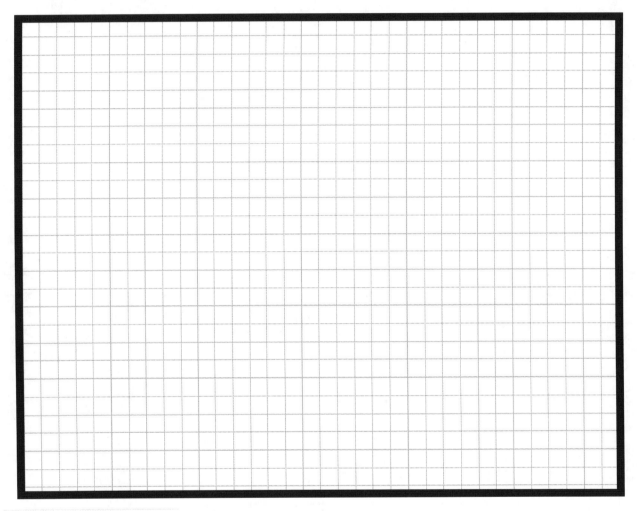

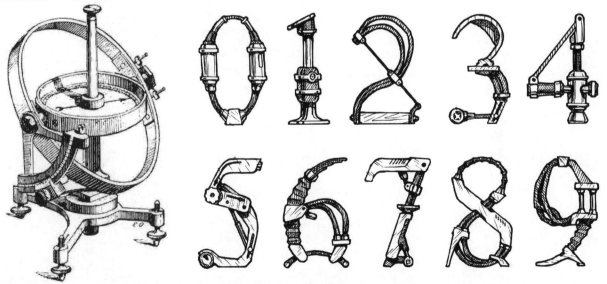

Listening Time

Listen to an audio book or classical music or ask someone to read a story to you while you color and draw on the next page.

What are you listening to?

_____

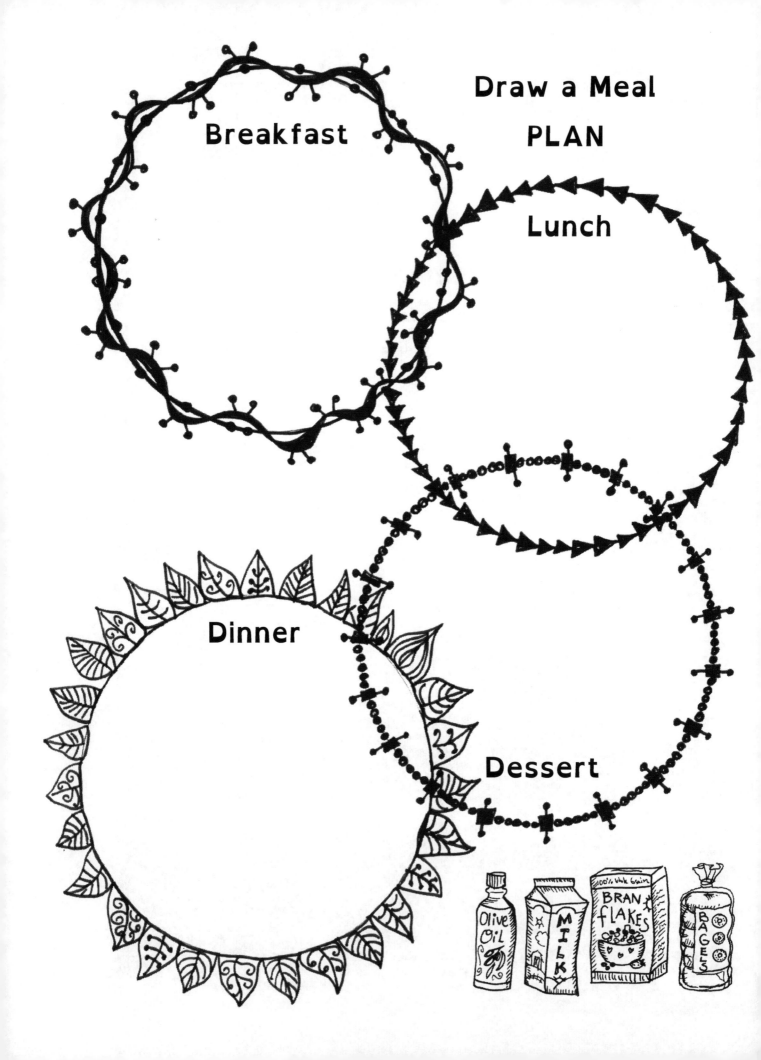

Breakfast

Draw a Meal
PLAN

Lunch

Dinner

Dessert

Circle Today's Date

January
February
March
April
May
June
July
August
September
October
November
December

1 2 3 4 5 6
7 8 9 10 11
12 13 14 15
16 17 18 19
20 21 22 23
24 25 26 27
28 29 30 31

MONDAY
TUESDAY
WEDNESDAY
THURSDAY
FRIDAY
SATURDAY
SUNDAY

2015
2016
2017
2018
2019
2020
2021
2022
2023
2024
2025
2026
2027
2028
2029

Write Today's Date: _____

Write down an inspirational quote:

My Goals

To-Do List

_____
_____
_____
_____
_____
_____

Observation Time

Look at the object in the picture.

Do you know what it is?

Yes / No / Unsure

Write down four facts or observations
about the object.

1. _____
2. _____
3. _____
4. _____

Emotions & Moods

How are your feeling today?
Color the facial expressions
to match today's moods.

Can you of three things that might help your mood improve?

1.
2.
3.

Nature Study

Go outside and make a realistic drawing of something you find in in nature.

Reading Time - 1 Hour

Choose Four Books - Read from each book for 15 minutes.

Copy a sentence or picture from each book here:

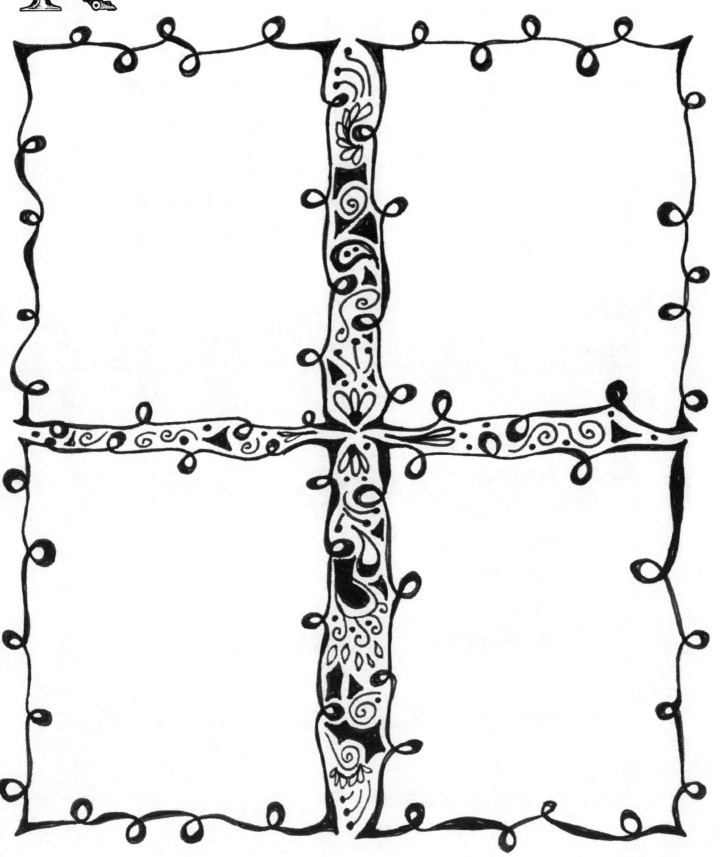

Circle Today's Date

January
February
March
April
May
June
July
August
September
October
November
December

1 2 3 4 5 6
7 8 9 10 11
12 13 14 15
16 17 18 19
20 21 22 23
24 25 26 27
28 29 30 31

MONDAY
TUESDAY
WEDNESDAY
THURSDAY
FRIDAY
SATURDAY
SUNDAY

2015
2016
2017
2018
2019
2020
2021
2022
2023
2024
2025
2026
2027
2028
2029

Write Today's Date: _ _ _ _ _ _ _ _ _ _ _ _ _ _ _

Spelling Time

Find 20 Words with 7 letters each.
Look in your books for words.
Write the words here:

Film Study

Watch a Documentary, Educational Program, Movie, or YouTube Tutorial.

TIME:

TITLE:

TOPIC: _____

I learned:_____

_____

_____

_____

NOTES:

Draw a Scene From the Film:

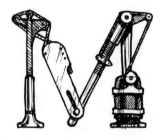

Math Practice

You can design something. You can make
graphs, maps, or geometric designs.
You can practice math problems.

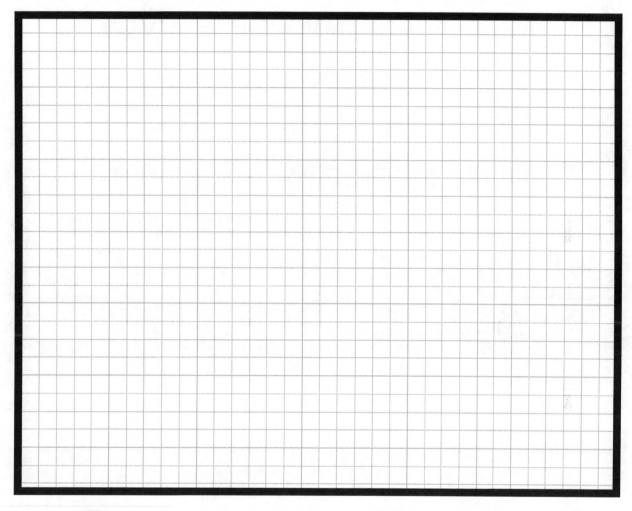

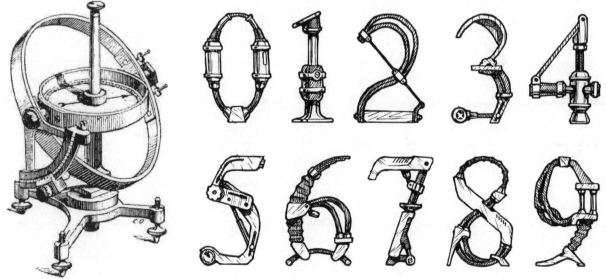

Fun Writing Practice:

ABCDEFGHIJKLMNOPQURSTUVWXYZ

abcdefghijklmnopqrstuvwxyz

ABCDEFGHIJKLMNOPQURSTUVWXYZ

ABCDEFGHIJKLMNOPQURSTUVWXYZ

abcdefghijklmnopqrstuvwxyz

Copywork

Find an interesting paragraph in one of your books and copy it. Be diligent to make your writing look exactly like it does the book.

TITLE:_____

Page Number:_____

_____

_____

_____

_____

_____

_____

_____

_____

_____

_____

Circle Today's Date

January
February
March
April
May
June
July
August
September
October
November
December

1 2 3 4 5 6
7 8 9 10 11
12 13 14 15
16 17 18 19
20 21 22 23
24 25 26 27
28 29 30 31

MONDAY
TUESDAY
WEDNESDAY
THURSDAY
FRIDAY
SATURDAY
SUNDAY

2015
2016
2017
2018
2019
2020
2021
2022
2023
2024
2025
2026
2027
2028
2029

Write Today's Date: _ _ _ _ _ _ _ _ _ _ _ _ _ _

Write down an inspirational quote:

My Goals

To-Do List

_____

_____

_____

_____

_____

_____

Creative Coloring Time

Emotions & Moods

How are your feeling today?
Color the facial expressions
to match today's moods.

Can you of three things that might help your mood improve?

1.
2.
3.

Nature Study

Go outside and make a realistic
drawing of something you find in
in nature.

Reading Time - 1 Hour

Choose Four Books - Read from each book for 15 minutes.

Copy a sentence or picture from each book here:

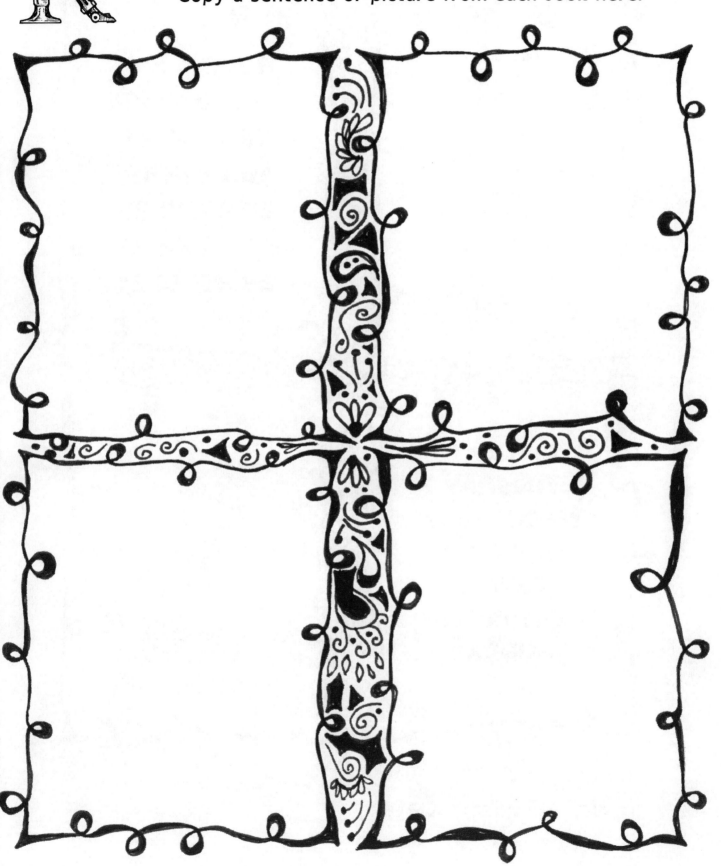

Circle Today's Date

January
February
March
April
May
June
July
August
September
October
November
December

1 2 3 4 5 6
7 8 9 10 11
12 13 14 15
16 17 18 19
20 21 22 23
24 25 26 27
28 29 30 31

MONDAY
TUESDAY
WEDNESDAY
THURSDAY
FRIDAY
SATURDAY
SUNDAY

2015
2016
2017
2018
2019
2020
2021
2022
2023
2024
2025
2026
2027
2028
2029

Write Today's Date: _ _ _ _ _ _ _ _ _ _ _ _ _ _ _

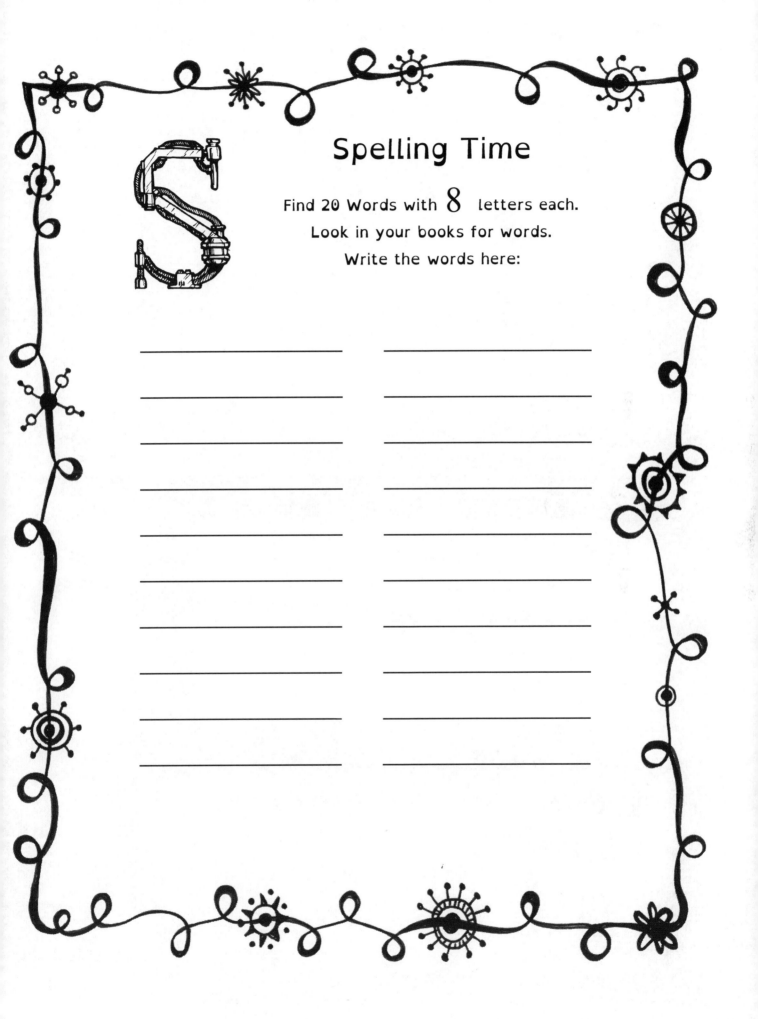

Spelling Time

Find 20 Words with 8 letters each.
Look in your books for words.
Write the words here:

Film Study

Watch a Documentary, Educational Program, Movie, or YouTube Tutorial.

TIME:

TITLE:

TOPIC: _____

I learned: _____

_____

_____

_____

NOTES:

Draw a Scene From the Film:

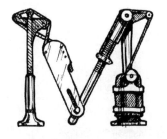

Math Practice

You can design something. You can make
graphs, maps, or geometric designs.
You can practice math problems.

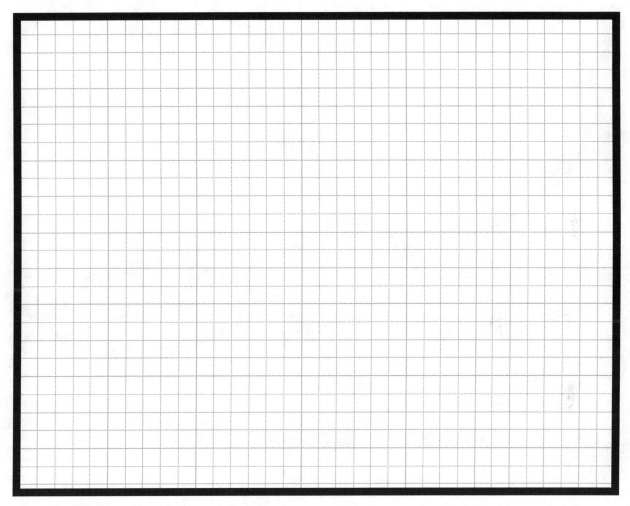

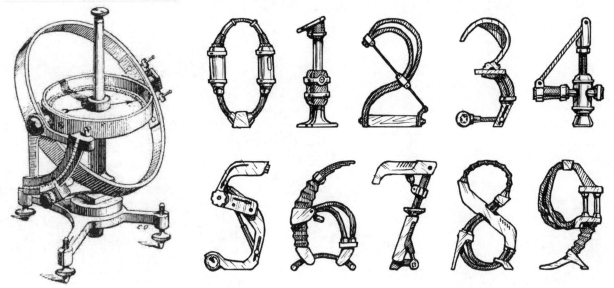

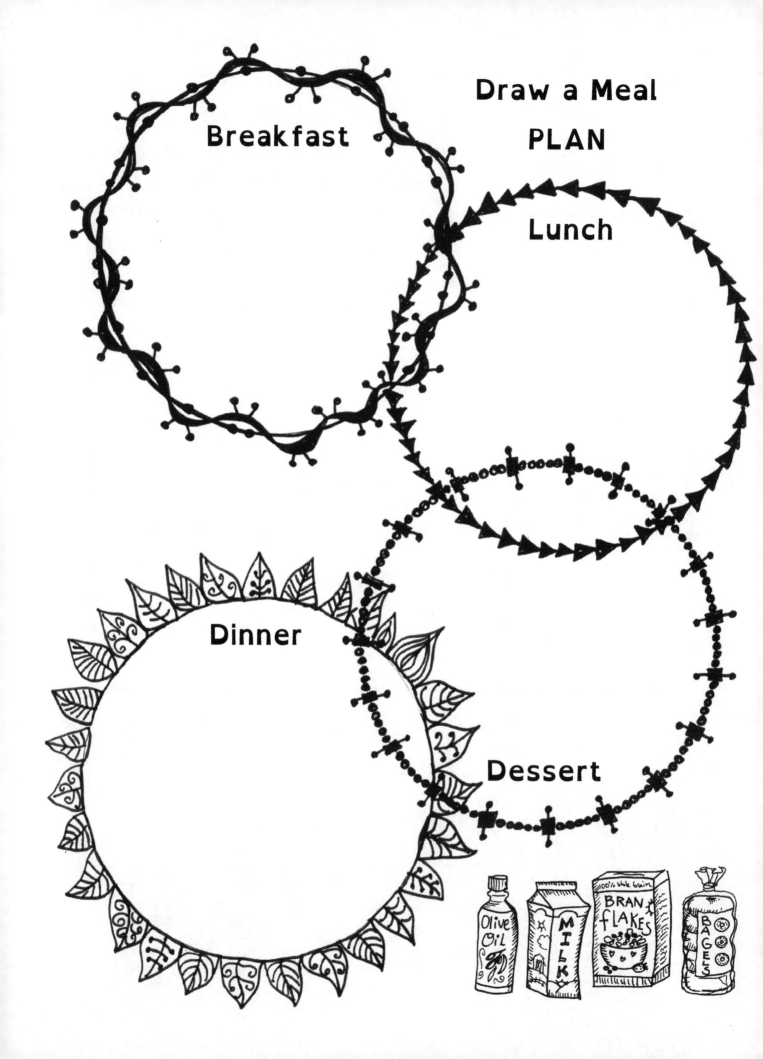

Copywork

Find an interesting paragraph in one of your books and copy it. Be diligent to make your writing look exactly like it does the book.

TITLE:_____

Page Number:_____

_____

_____

_____

_____

_____

_____

_____

_____

_____

 Creative
Coloring Time

Circle Today's Date

January
February
March
April
May
June
July
August
September
October
November
December

1 2 3 4 5 6
7 8 9 10 11
12 13 14 15
16 17 18 19
20 21 22 23
24 25 26 27
28 29 30 31

MONDAY
TUESDAY
WEDNESDAY
THURSDAY
FRIDAY
SATURDAY
SUNDAY

2015
2016
2017
2018
2019
2020
2021
2022
2023
2024
2025
2026
2027
2028
2029

Write Today's Date: _____

Write down an inspirational quote:

My Goals

To-Do List

_____
_____
_____
_____
_____
_____

Emotions & Moods

How are your feeling today?
Color the facial expressions
to match today's moods.

Can you of three things that might help your mood improve?

1.
2.
3.

Nature Study

Go outside and make a realistic
drawing of something you find in
in nature.

Reading Time - 1 Hour

Choose Four Books - Read from each book for 15 minutes.

Copy a sentence or picture from each book here:

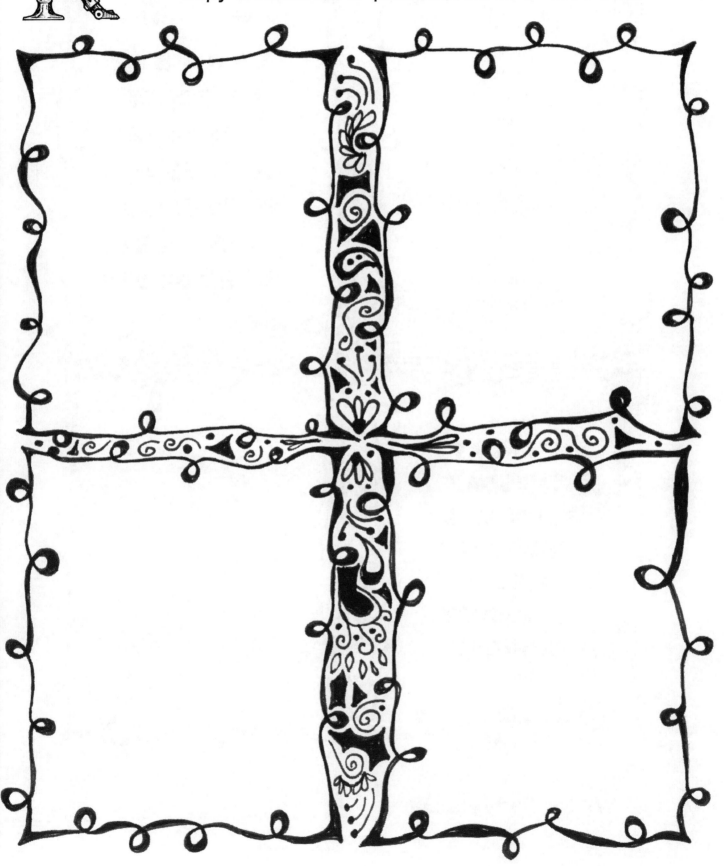

Circle Today's Date

January
February
March
April
May
June
July
August
September
October
November
December

1 2 3 4 5 6
7 8 9 10 11
12 13 14 15
16 17 18 19
20 21 22 23
24 25 26 27
28 29 30 31

MONDAY
TUESDAY
WEDNESDAY
THURSDAY
FRIDAY
SATURDAY
SUNDAY

2015
2016
2017
2018
2019
2020
2021
2022
2023
2024
2025
2026
2027
2028
2029

Write Today's Date: _ _ _ _ _ _ _ _ _ _ _ _ _ _

Film Study

Watch a Documentary, Educational Program, Movie, or YouTube Tutorial.

TITLE:

TIME:

TOPIC: _____

I learned: _____

_____

_____

_____

NOTES:

Draw a Scene From the Film:

Spelling Time

Find 20 Words with **7** letters each.
Look in your books for words.
Write the words here:

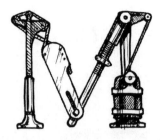

Math Practice

You can design something. You can make
graphs, maps, or geometric designs.
You can practice math problems.

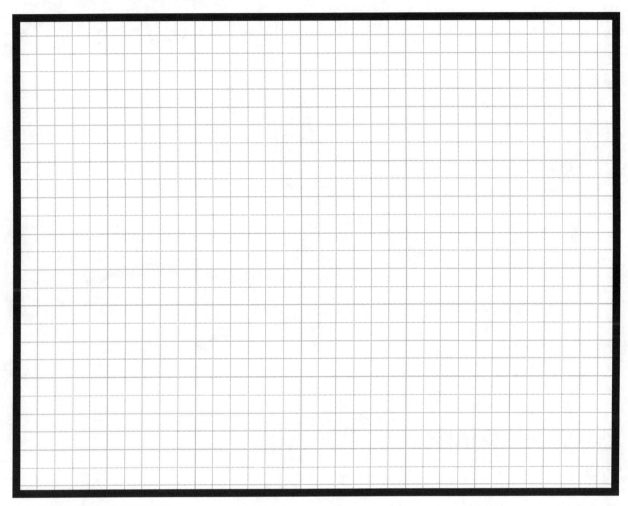

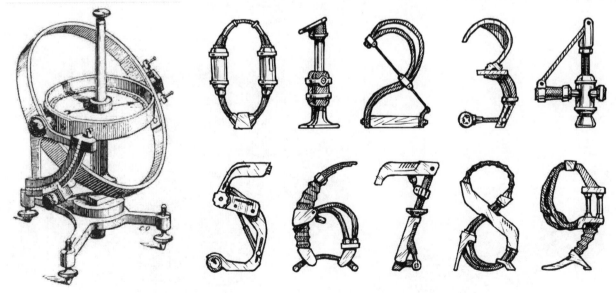

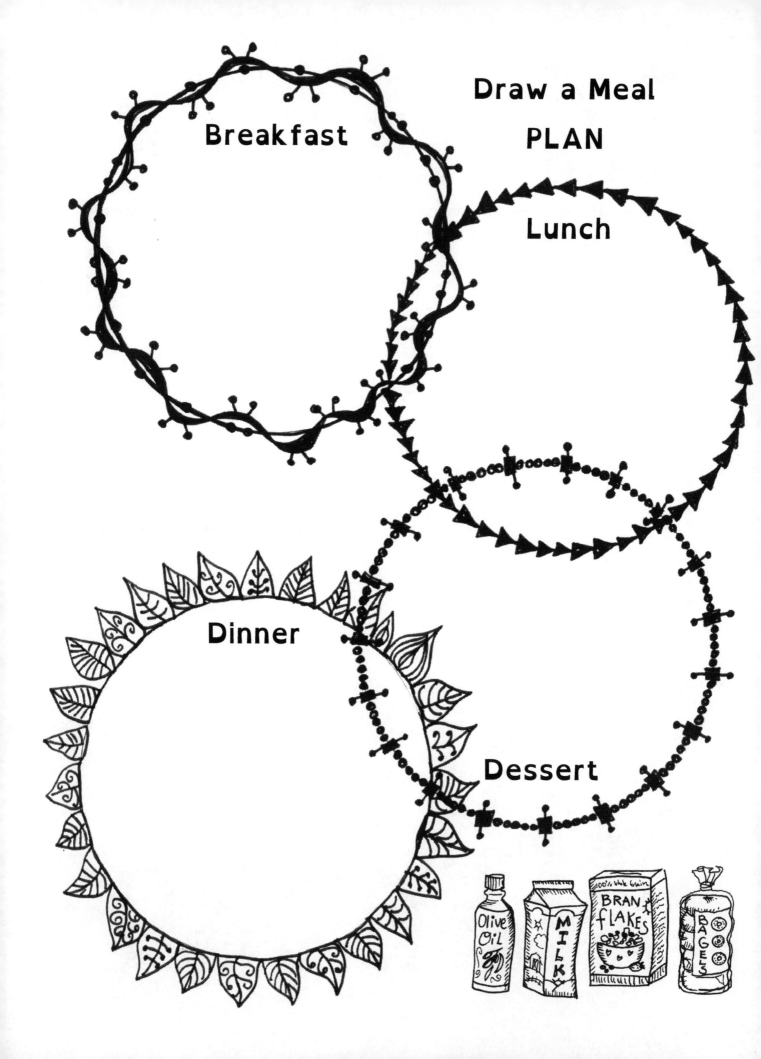

Copywork

Find an interesting paragraph in one of your books and copy it. Be diligent to make your writing look exactly like it does the book.

TITLE:_____

Page Number:_____

_____

_____

_____

_____

_____

_____

_____

_____

_____

 Creative
Coloring Time

Circle Today's Date

January
February
March
April
May
June
July
August
September
October
November
December

1 2 3 4 5 6
7 8 9 10 11
12 13 14 15
16 17 18 19
20 21 22 23
24 25 26 27
28 29 30 31

MONDAY
TUESDAY
WEDNESDAY
THURSDAY
FRIDAY
SATURDAY
SUNDAY

2015
2016
2017
2018
2019
2020
2021
2022
2023
2024
2025
2026
2027
2028
2029

Write Today's Date: _ _ _ _ _ _ _ _ _ _ _ _ _ _ _

Write down an inspirational quote:

My Goals

To-Do List

_____
_____
_____
_____
_____
_____

Nature Study

Go outside and make a realistic
drawing of something you find in
in nature.

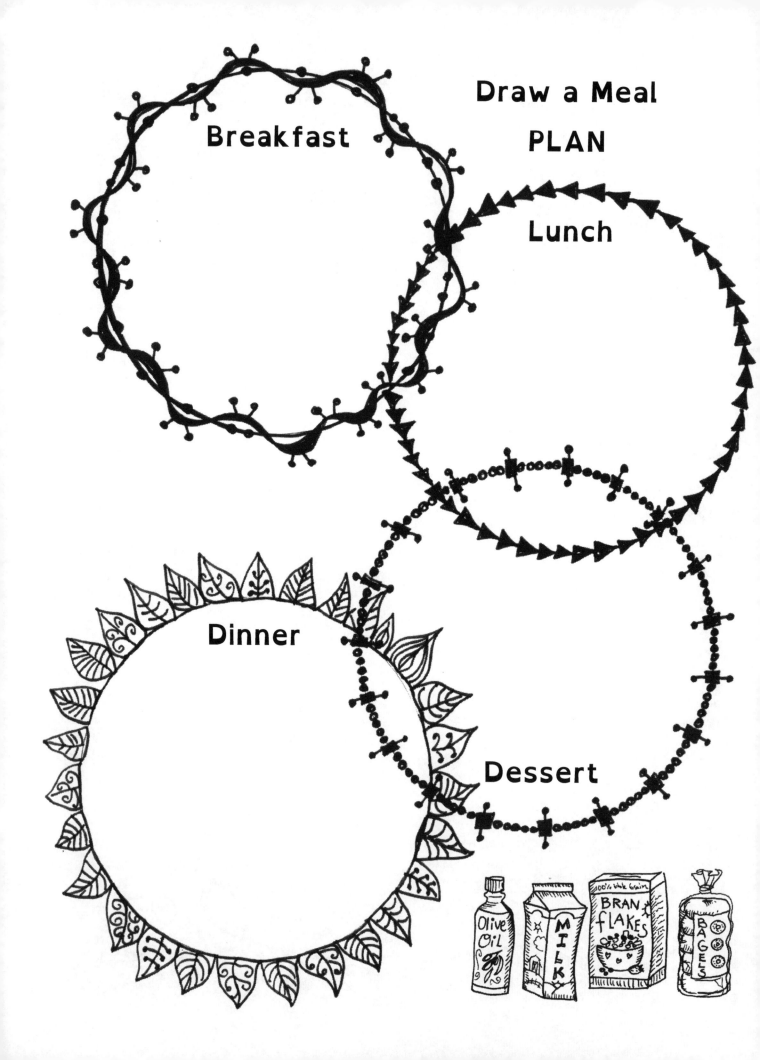

Draw a Meal
PLAN

Breakfast

Lunch

Dinner

Dessert

Reading Time - 1 Hour

Choose Four Books - Read from each book for 15 minutes.

Copy a sentence or picture from each book here:

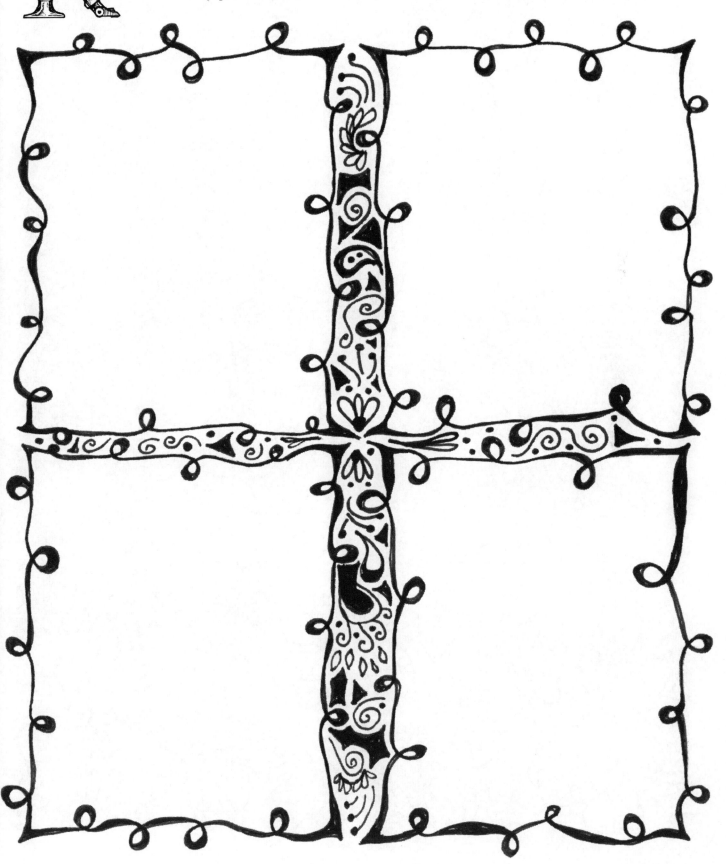

Circle Today's Date

January
February
March
April
May
June
July
August
September
October
November
December

1 2 3 4 5 6
7 8 9 10 11
12 13 14 15
16 17 18 19
20 21 22 23
24 25 26 27
28 29 30 31

MONDAY
TUESDAY
WEDNESDAY
THURSDAY
FRIDAY
SATURDAY
SUNDAY

2015
2016
2017
2018
2019
2020
2021
2022
2023
2024
2025
2026
2027
2028
2029

Write Today's Date: _ _ _ _ _ _ _ _ _ _ _ _ _ _ _

Spelling Time

Find 20 Words with 7 letters each.
Look in your books for words.
Write the words here:

_____   _____

_____   _____

_____   _____

_____   _____

_____   _____

_____   _____

_____   _____

_____   _____

_____   _____

Film Study

Watch a Documentary, Educational Program, Movie, or YouTube Tutorial.

TIME:

TITLE:

TOPIC: _____

I learned:_____

_____

_____

_____

NOTES:

Draw a Scene From the Film:

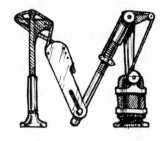

Math Practice

You can design something. You can make
graphs, maps, or geometric designs.
You can practice math problems.

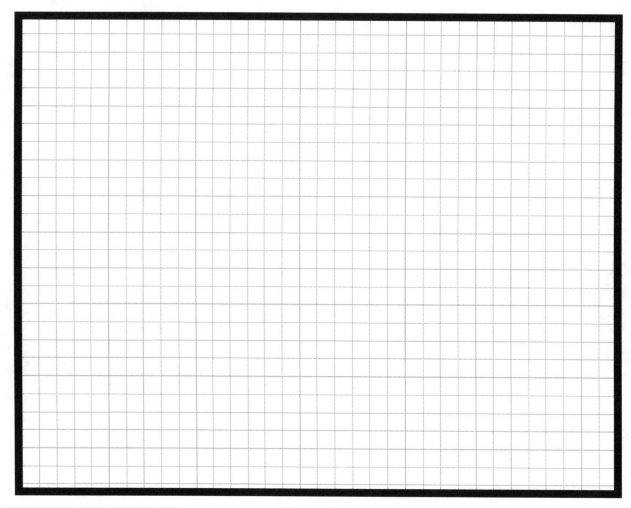

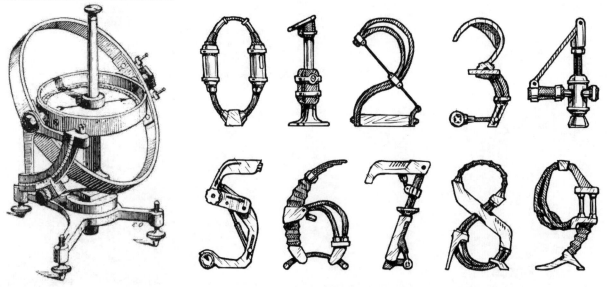

Copywork

Find an interesting paragraph in one of your books and copy it. Be diligent to make your writing look exactly like it does the book.

TITLE:_____

Page Number:_____

_____

_____

_____

_____

_____

_____

_____

_____

_____

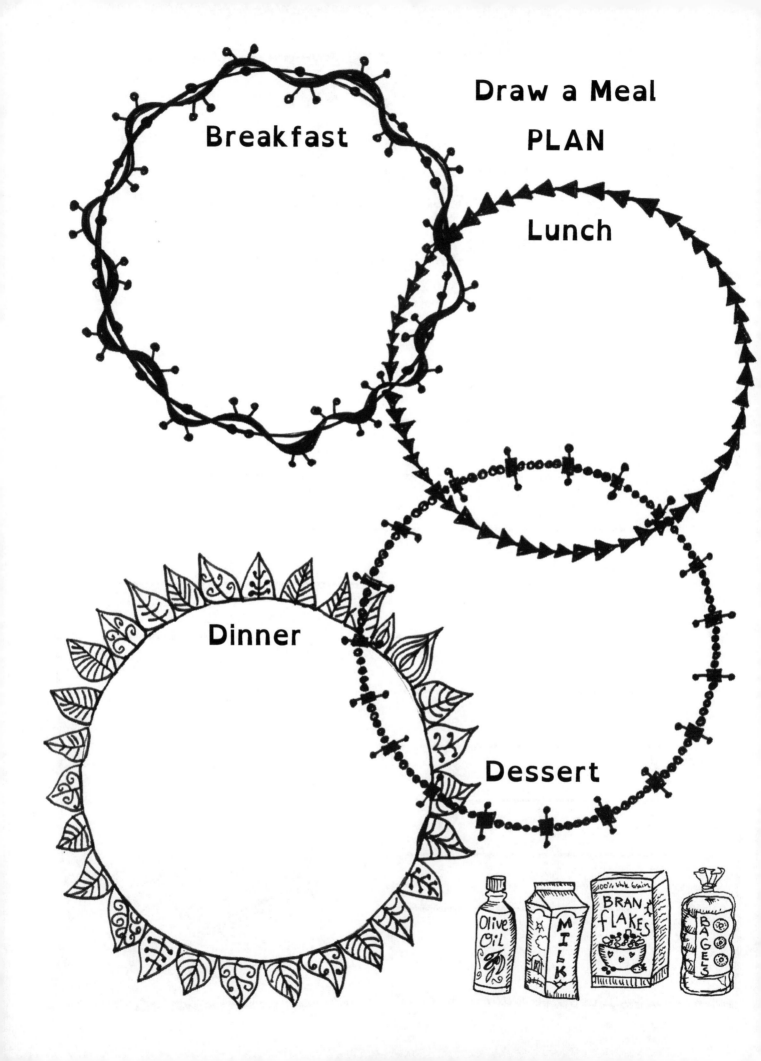

Breakfast

Draw a Meal
PLAN

Lunch

Dinner

Dessert

Circle Today's Date

January
February
March
April
May
June
July
August
September
October
November
December

1 2 3 4 5 6
7 8 9 10 11
12 13 14 15
16 17 18 19
20 21 22 23
24 25 26 27
28 29 30 31

MONDAY
TUESDAY
WEDNESDAY
THURSDAY
FRIDAY
SATURDAY
SUNDAY

2015
2016
2017
2018
2019
2020
2021
2022
2023
2024
2025
2026
2027
2028
2029

Write Today's Date: _ _ _ _ _ _ _ _ _ _ _ _ _ _ _ _ _

Write down an inspirational quote:

My Goals

To-Do List

_____
_____
_____
_____
_____
_____

Emotions & Moods

How are your feeling today?
Color the facial expressions
to match today's moods.

Can you of three things that might help your mood improve?

1.
2.
3.

Nature Study

Go outside and make a realistic drawing of something you find in in nature.

Reading Time - 1 Hour

Choose Four Books - Read from each book for 15 minutes.

Copy a sentence or picture from each book here:

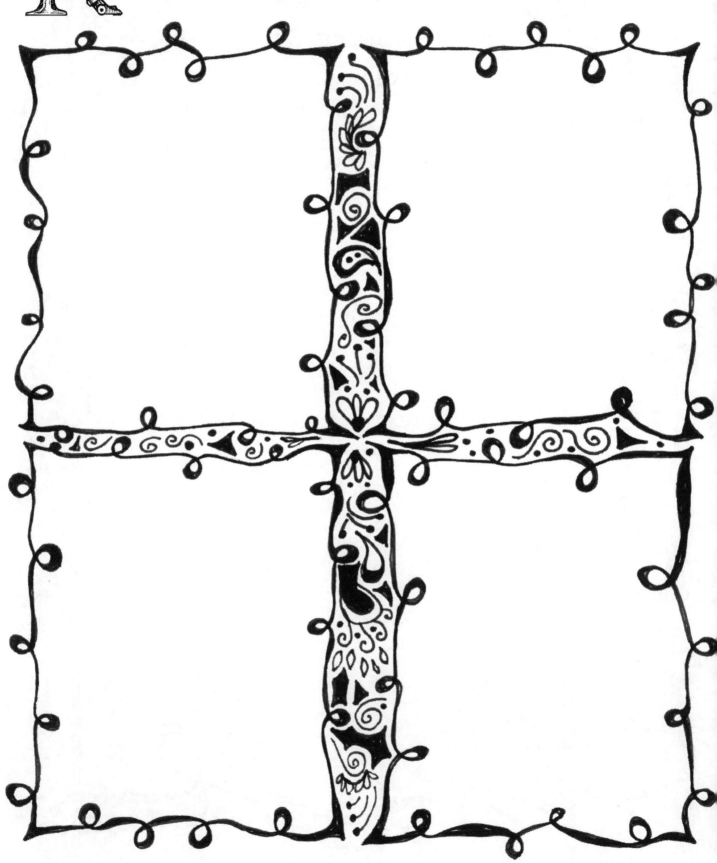

Circle Today's Date

January
February
March
April
May
June
July
August
September
October
November
December

1 2 3 4 5 6
7 8 9 10 11
12 13 14 15
16 17 18 19
20 21 22 23
24 25 26 27
28 29 30 31

MONDAY
TUESDAY
WEDNESDAY
THURSDAY
FRIDAY
SATURDAY
SUNDAY

2015
2016
2017
2018
2019
2020
2021
2022
2023
2024
2025
2026
2027
2028
2029

Write Today's Date: _ _ _ _ _ _ _ _ _ _ _ _ _ _ _ _ _

Spelling Time

S

Find 20 Words with 10 letters each.
Look in your books for words.
Write the words here:

_____   _____

_____   _____

_____   _____

_____   _____

_____   _____

_____   _____

_____   _____

_____   _____

_____   _____

Film Study

Watch a Documentary, Educational Program, Movie, or YouTube Tutorial.

TITLE:

TIME:

TOPIC: _____

I learned: _____

_____

_____

_____

NOTES:

Draw a Scene From the Film:

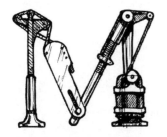

Math Practice

You can design something. You can make
graphs, maps, or geometric designs.
You can practice math problems.

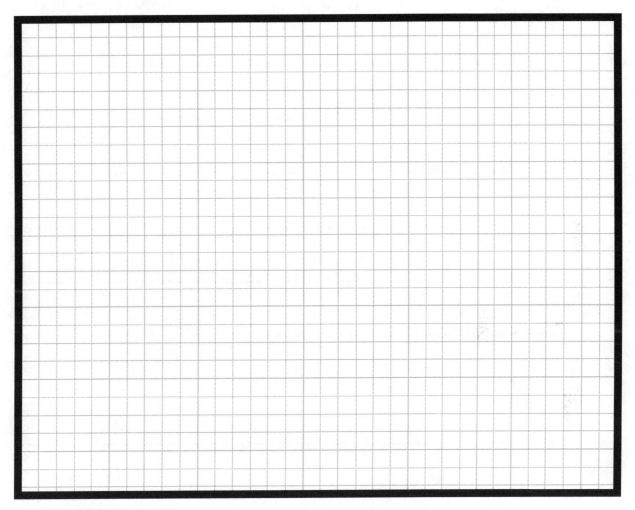

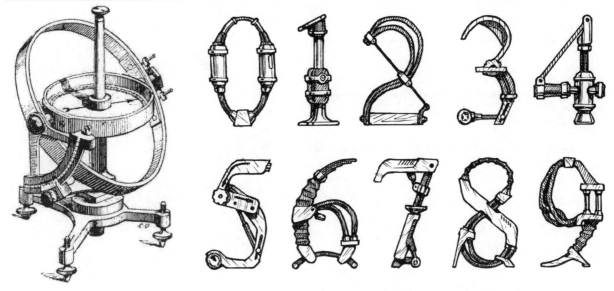

Copywork

Find an interesting paragraph in one of your books and copy it. Be diligent to make your writing look exactly like it does the book.

TITLE:_____

Page Number:_____

_____

_____

_____

_____

_____

_____

_____

_____

_____

Fun Writing Practice:

ABCDEFGHIJKLMNOPQURSTUVWXYZ

abcdefghijklmnopqrstuvwxyz

ABCDEFGHIJKLMNOPQURSTUVWXYZ

ABCDEFGHIJKLMNOPQURSTUVWXYZ

abcdefghijklmnopqrstuvwxyz

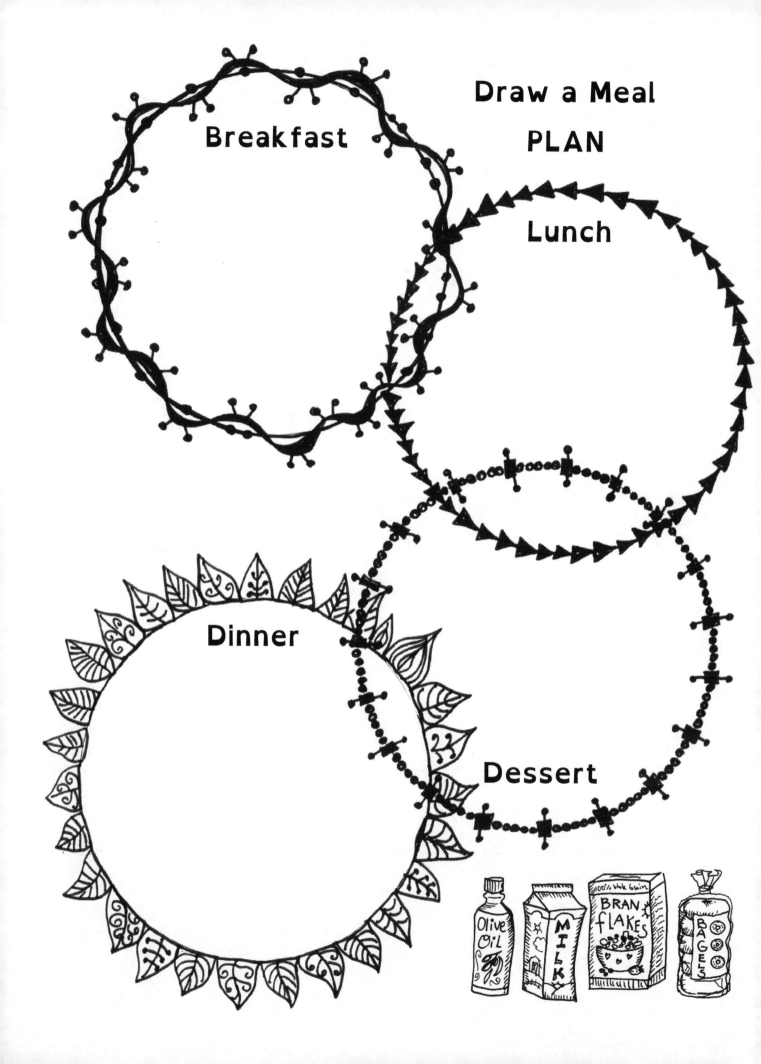

Draw a Meal PLAN

Breakfast

Lunch

Dinner

Dessert

Do It Yourself
HOMESCHOOL
JOURNALS

Copyright Information

Contact Us:

The Thinking Tree LLC
617 N. Swope St. Greenfield, IN 46140. United States
317.622.8852 PHONE (Dial +1 outside of the USA) 267.712.7889 FAX
www.DyslexiaGames.com
jbrown@DyslexiaGames.com